A SURVIVAL GUIDE FOR TOUGH TIMES

Mike Phillips

Bethany Fellowship INC.
MINNEAPOLIS, MINNESOTA 55438

Published by Bethany Fellowship, Inc.
6820 Auto Club Road, Minneapolis, Mn. 55438

Printed in the United States of America

Library of Congress Cataloging in Publication Data

Phillips, Mike, 1946—
    A survival guide for tough times.

    Bibliography: p:
    1. Christian life—1960-   2. Family—
Religious life.   3. Human ecology—Moral and religious
aspects.   4. End of the world.   I.   Title.
BV4501.2P53   248'.4   79-4261
ISBN 0-87123-498-X

DEDICATION

To my sons,
Robin
Patrick
Gregory

and to my father,
Denver Phillips

ABOUT THE AUTHOR

Mike Phillips was raised in a Christian home in Arcata, California. He graduated from Humboldt State University with a degree in Physics and Math in 1969. He began a part-time book-selling effort which branched into what are presently two large bookstores in Eureka and Santa Rosa.

Phillips married in 1971, and he and his wife, Judy, have three children. Judy does the accounting for the bookstore business. Mike confesses to being an ardent fan of C. S. Lewis' writings and a track "nut." He runs several miles every morning.

Other books by Mike Philllips are: *A Christian Family in Action, Growth of a Vision, Does Christianity Make Sense?, Blueprint for Raising a Child,* and *Control Through Planned Budgeting—A Management Guide for Christian Bookstores.*

ACKNOWLEDGMENTS

I would like to publicly recognize two people whose diligence in our bookstore has allowed me to work on this and other writing projects. They are Maxine Campbell and Michael McClure. Words cannot tell how thankful to God I am for them. In addition to very skillfully managing the store, Michael (along with my wife, Judy) also serves as one of my most encouraging, yet ruthless, critics. This, as any writer knows, is invaluable if a manuscript is ever to find its way into print. I thank Michael and Judy for this stimulating, disheartening, motivating, and extremely essential help as well.

Let us, then, as Christians rejoice that we see around us on every hand the decay of the institutions and instruments of power; intimations of empires falling to pieces, money in total disarray, dictators and parliamentarians alike nonplussed by the confusion and conflicts which encompass them. For it is precisely when every earthly hope has been explored and found wanting, when every possibility of help from earthly sources has been sought and is not forthcoming, when every recourse this world offers, moral as well as material, has been explored to no effect, when in the shivering cold the last faggot has been thrown on the fire and in the gathering darkness every glimmer of light has finally flickered out—it is then that Christ's hand reaches out, sure and firm, that Christ's words bring their inexpressible comfort, that his light shines brightest, abolishing the darkness for ever. So, *finding in everything only deception and nothingness, the soul is constrained to have recourse to God himself and to rest content with him.*

—Malcolm Muggeridge
Christ and the Media
Wm. B. Eerdmans Publishing Co.

CONTENTS

INTRODUCTION

This is a book about the future. It is not, however, what I would call a "prophecy" book. In it I do not intend to prophesy concerning what I think will take place in the future. There are enough books, theories, and prognostications around already without my adding another. I want you to understand right now—this is not the definitive prophecy book.

But we are going to discuss the future, though it will be in a way that is probably new to you. We are going to look at ways we can prepare for the future *whatever it happens to hold*—no matter which particular theory turns out to be the final way world events and God's plan blend together in the coming years. The principles in this book are not contingent on some specific hypothesis which seeks to accurately detail coming events.

In so saying I do not mean to imply that this book is not written from a particular point of view. It is. But this point of view is largely general rather than specific. And this general thesis is simply that world events are on a collision course with God's plan for the future. In many respects the world systems are falling apart. All indications are that conditions will continue to become worse—from population explosion to pollution to energy problems to food shortages to crime to decaying morality. And it is my belief that Christians will be right in the thick of these increasing problems and hardships. Scriptures seems to indicate that God will allow His people to remain through at least some tribulation and persecution. This will have two purposes: to purify us as a people who are being made ready for the return of Jesus and to allow us to minister love and healing to the people of the world.

Whether or not we will actually be present on the earth during "The Great Tribulation" I do not know. This is an area of prophetic speculation in which I simply do not have any theory I can wholeheartedly embrace. The same is true concerning the Rapture and all sorts of other eschatological events, timetables, wars, and locations. Though such topics have occupied the pens of prophetic writers for years, I personally do not feel that knowing these things precisely is my prime responsibility. My priority must be to live like Jesus did in a world hopelessly in need of God's love.

We've all seen charts that detail the future and have read books that spell out events, chronologies and strategies. Many of these charts and books by well-qualified authors, though carefully researched and supported by various scriptures, do not coincide in specific conclusions. So I find myself reluctant to endorse any particular prediction beyond some general ideas about where the world is headed. My specific plans for preparation, therefore, are based on one of the general themes most prophetic writers hold in common: hardship is coming to the world and Christians must prepare for it. But if events don't occur as we think they might, these suggestions will equip us for ministry right now.

What makes these principles exciting is that they prepare us in two ways. If Christians are to be included in some of the frightening things that Scripture indicates are coming to the world, then these measures will prepare us for them. But should the future turn out completely different than any of us have imagined, and even if Jesus should not return to earth for years and years, these efforts still will enable us to live more productive, fruitful, ministering lives in the meantime.

Realistically speaking, it is good for us to be aware of the wide deviation in opinion about the future even though we might not have come to final conclusions ourselves. My recent inclination has been to assume that these are the end times. Hal Lindsay and many others write that this is so and even have predicted the Lord's return within twenty or thirty years. And though this viewpoint has been an integral part of my own spiritual diet, I must recognize that all scholarly authorities are not in agreement. William Barclay talks about continuing to live and work as a Christian with little thought for Jesus' immediate return. And other writers occupy every point on the spectrum between.

Concerning the nature of the persecution to come, there is much divergent opinion as well. Lindsay and Kirban and a host of other well-known writers maintain that Christians will not be present on earth when the most severe and widespread persecution and tribulation begin. David Wilkerson, on the other hand, says, "I am just one of many in this nation who now warn Americans to get ready for persecution and judgment." [1]

In spite of our personal beliefs on any certain aspect of biblical prophecy, I believe that we need to build into our attitude a certain flexibility which is willing to consider differing views. Now let me be very plain here: there are certain basic doctrines of Christianity which are clearly set forth in Scripture—sin, the atonement, repentance, conversion, etc. And the doctrine of Christ's coming again to earth is unmistakably obvious. I am not advocating some kind of weak broadmindedness concerning explicit Christian truths. But at the same time, it is imperative that we do not base our way of living on our particular eschatological stance. It is enough that we prepare ourselves for hardship and deprivation. Beyond that general prediction I choose not to go.

In a sense this book is divided into two sections. The first, entitled "What Can We Expect in the Coming Years?" is almost testimonial. It deals with how I came to be interested in prophecy and how that interest led me over the years to seek a life-style which would train me to live productively in the days I was sure were coming. The specifics of that mode of life—from eating habits to exercise to working with my hands to how I spend my money—is what the second section, the remainder of the book, is about. At first glance this book may seem like a potpourri of subjects, all unrelated—certainly unrelated to the future. But after you have finished the book I think you'll agree that our approach to these many and varied aspects of daily life has everything to do with our personal preparation for the days ahead.

You may find yourself having to shift gears as you read. One moment we will be discussing a Bible prophecy and then right on to financial matters, unity within the body of God's people, or losing weight. The reason for this is that we have become accustomed to rigidly categorizing our thoughts and spiritual study, rarely allowing for overlap and interplay. This book will be different. We will be discussing preparation for the future in terms of activities you probably have never considered in light of prophecy. This especially will be true as you move into Part II. Please bear in mind that the first section simply provides the foundational background for the remainder of the book.

One final, very important note. The suggestions in the chapters that follow are not intended as any sort of spirituality measurement. Some of these things may have no relevance to your life whatever. That's all right. Take what you can use, and don't allow the parts which don't apply to sidetrack you. In these issues, each Christian must be sensitive to the Spirit within. There very likely will be areas I don't even mention where God is specifically at work in your life.

One of my goals in writing this book is not to be legalistic about the exact methods of preparation but to stimulate thought about the kind of Christian God wants today. Though admittedly many of the suggestions here are specific, let the Lord use this approach to show you other ways to prepare as well. This is but the beginning.

PART I

WHAT CAN WE EXPECT IN THE COMING YEARS?

1

A Talk by a Man Named Lindsay

The Southern California orange groves are intoxicating in late summer. As we drove through San Bernardino and up the mountain toward Arrowhead Springs, I breathed in the smells with relish.

The mood was set. I knew God was going to do some exciting things in the coming week.

I had just returned from a summer abroad working with a German family on their farm. It had been a good three months. And now I was on my way to a discipleship training camp at the headquarters for Campus Crusade for Christ.

"What a perfect way to top off the summer and start the new school year," I thought to myself as we wound our way up the mountain.

And I was not disappointed.

Though the first several days were enjoyable, it was not until Thursday that I heard what would be for me the pivotal talk of the entire week. In the Wednesday dinner line I chanced to overhear two students talking in front of me.

"Have you heard 'The Generation of the Fig Tree' yet?" the girl asked her companion.

"No, I don't think so," said the other. "At least I don't remember it."

I quickly glanced down at my schedule and saw that the Fig Tree lecture was scheduled for the following night. I had heard nothing about it until now.

"You'd know if you had," the first girl continued. "It isn't a talk you'll soon forget. I was at another conference last week. I heard it then."

"What's it all about?" her friend asked.

"Oh, I wouldn't want to spoil it for you. But a lot of things in your life will change as a result of it; that much I will say."

"Who's the speaker?"

"Lindsay," she said.

They moved on and I was left wondering what made Lindsay's talk so unusual and what the generation of the fig tree was all about.

Of course today most informed Christians would immediately recognize the name Hal Lindsay and would have a pretty good idea that the subject of his talk might well be biblical prophecy.

But in 1967 it was different. It would be three years before Lindsay's best-selling book *The Late Great Planet Earth* would first hit the nation's bookshelves. Prophecy was still a sleeping giant. While many Christians had studied the books of Revelation and Daniel, there was nothing resembling the enormous wave of interest and hundreds of books on the subject that exists today.

And though I had been brought up as a Christian, "prophecy" was a foreign word to me. I had not the slightest knowledge about *anything* related to coming events. I had never heard that world events were following a biblical pattern and timetable. The terms "rapture," "second coming," "tribulation," and "millennium" were virtually unknown to me.

As I walked into the outdoor amphitheater the following evening my mind was completely blank. I had no idea what to expect.

I sat back and waited.

Of course I knew vaguely that much of the Bible had to do with prophecy of the future. I had been taught that the Old Testament foretold many New Testament events as they actually happened. But I hadn't known that more than half the prophecies concerning Christ are as yet unfulfilled and that students of biblical prophecy are anxiously anticipating their completion within a very few years.

My interest began to mount even further when Lindsay said, "There seems to be something unique about this time we are living in, because we are starting to witness the fulfillment of many of these prophecies *today*."

He listed for us example after example of events found in current magazines and newspapers that coincide remarkably with prophetic revelations found in the Bible. According to Lindsay, the scriptures predict everything from UFO's to increased earthquakes to rampant sin to the rise in the occult.

Then he moved his attention to the nation of Israel and showed how some remarkable prophecies from the Bible, over two thousand years old, are now actually happening. After nearly 2000 years of exile and relentless persecution, the Jewish people became a nation again in 1948.

"But what are all these events leading up to? That is the crucial question. Why are these things all happening *now*?"

To answer his own question, Lindsay looked at the discussion between Jesus and His disciples when they asked Him, "What will be the sign of your coming?" In reply Jesus gave many general signs that would be prevalent in the world before He would return—religious apostasy, wars, national revolutions, earthquakes, famines, etc.—things Lindsay had already shown to be happening increasingly in our time.

"Now many of you," he continued, "may be unfamiliar with the term 'second coming.' But it simply refers to the second time when Jesus will come to the earth. From this discussion with His disciples it is clear Jesus was giving them evidence to watch for, events which would precede that time. He speaks of these signs as 'birth pangs,' implying they would increase in frequency and intensity up until the moment of His return. Two of the most important such signs (which in years past Bible students were unable to fit into the prophetic puzzle) are the restoration of the Jewish people in the land of Palestine and the rebuilding of the Temple in Jerusalem on its original site.

"As we mentioned before, in 1948 Israel once again became a nation. World events seem to fulfill Jesus' words daily: very recently the Israeli army recaptured Jerusalem, and just recently discussions began in Jerusalem about the reconstruction of the Temple. Yes, Jesus is returning to earth; that is what world events are leading up to. And these fulfilled prophecies seem to indicate it could be soon. The countdown is underway. The birth pangs have begun."

By this time I was practically out of my seat. I'd never heard anything like this in my life! I had never known Jesus was to return to earth again. "I just can't believe it," I thought to myself. "Imagine! Jesus is actually coming back to earth!"

But Hal Lindsay was not through yet. The best was yet to come.

"Not only are the events themselves happening in fulfillment of scripture, Jesus himself gives a very important time clue, a clue that if properly understood can actually help pinpoint the time when the culmination of these things will take place."

Every one of us in that auditorium were on the edge of our seats. There wasn't a sound as we hung on every word.

"For thousands of years," Lindsay said, "God's people have looked forward to the day when Jesus would return. But it has not happened yet. All these people have gone to their graves still looking for the return of the Lord. But for a certain generation it will not be so. There will be a people on the earth when He does come. And Jesus himself gives us the clue how we can determine who that people will be. Listen to His words:

> Learn a lesson from the fig-tree. When its tender shoots appear and are breaking into leaf, you know that summer is near. In the same way, when you see all this happening, you may know that the end is

near, at the very door. (Mark 13:28-29, NEB)

"Remember the signs we have seen. When these signs begin to multiply and increase in scope, it is similar to the fig tree putting forth its leaves. And when that happens, summer is just around the corner. Jesus says when these signs become visible, He is right at the door. Keep in mind too that the fig tree has traditionally been a historical symbol of the nation of Israel. So when the Jewish people became a nation again in 1948, the fig tree in a sense put forth its first leaves. And the signs like birth pangs ever since confirm that the leaves are indeed increasing in number and that summer is near. Jesus' return, therefore, is near, right at the door.

"And listen to His final promise," Lindsay continued; " 'Truly I say to you, *this generation shall not pass away* till all these things be done.' What generation is Jesus speaking of? Obviously, in context, the generation that would see the signs—chief among them the rebirth of Israel.

"Now a generation in the Bible is something like forty years. If this then is a correct deduction, within forty or so years of 1948 all these things could take place. Many scholars who have studied Bible prophecy all their lives believe this is so. [2] It is, therefore, *this generation* of whom Jesus is speaking. This is the generation that has seen the fig tree put forth its leaves. It is *you and I* Jesus was talking about. *We* are the generation of the fig tree. You are the people who will see the time when these things will be fulfilled.

"From everything I can tell from my study of the scriptures, Jesus will return to earth in your lifetime."

Lindsay walked from the podium.

The talk was over, yet the crowd sat stunned. Silence hung over us. I was not the only one to have been deeply affected.

Slowly and quietly people began to get up from their seats and make their way out.

I remained in my seat a few moments longer.

"In my lifetime," I thought. I could scarcely believe what I'd heard.

"In *my* lifetime!"

It All Fits Together

When the week was over and I began the long eight-hundred-mile drive home with my friends, I could hardly focus my attention on anything but Lindsay's talk. I sat in the car for miles at a time reading and underlining in the Book of the Revelation.

When I arrived home I reviewed my notes of his talk and continued to look up passages in my Bible. I read the books I had bought at the conference and several of us studied together for a time, trying to fit the pieces of the prophetic picture together into some sort of unified pattern. The fact that began gradually to come into focus was that these future events Lindsay had described were not isolated but fit perfectly into God's overall plan and purpose for the world.

What I had never previously been aware of was that there had always been dual facets to the character of Jesus, both of which would one day be fully demonstrated and fulfilled. Jesus' first entry into the world as a man demonstrated His loving and humble servanthood, willing to submit to death for us. But Jesus' coming to the earth as a conquering and reigning King was yet to be fulfilled. I had always thought this would take place in heaven. Now I saw that it would be fulfilled when Jesus returned again to earth. The world, therefore, is still waiting to see the final fulfillment of God's victory over Satan by His Son. The return of Jesus is the hinge upon which all of the future turns.

And the more I read the more the evidence seemed to mount, saying, "These final events are rapidly approaching. The time is imminent!"

One of the most intriguing bits of evidence of all was the approach of the year 2000. Had there been no other confirmations whatsoever, this one single item would have been enough to convince me that Jesus' return was near. For every 2000 years there has been some spiritually cataclysmic event in God's dealing with the universe which has, each time, changed the course of history from that moment on for all time. Approximately six thousand years ago, God created Adam. Two thousand years later, God forever altered His relationship with the men He had created by making a covenant with Abraham which would stand forever. Two thousand years after that God sent His Son Jesus to earth to die for our sins. We are now on the verge of another two-thousand-year span. And the next major event in the timetable of God's plan is the return of Jesus to the earth. Certainly the prophecies being fulfilled all about us in the world today indicate we are approaching that time.

To add to these facts is the principle woven throughout Scripture of six days of work followed by a day of rest. God created in this manner and commanded man to live according to the same pattern. But we are also told that with God a day is just as a thousand years and a thousand years is as a day (2 Peter 3:8). Since man has now been on the earth approximately six thousand years, God has in a sense "labored" over him for six "days." Is it unreasonable to conclude then that a day of rest is coming? A time of peace on the earth? If so, the thousand-year millennium, during which Jesus is to reign on the earth, begins to fit perfectly into the whole pattern. And it seems all the more near.

My Bible study and reading continued to excite me as these things dawned on me one at a time. But there was a gloomy side I had to face as well. Because I also read that before Jesus does return to earth, God is going to allow Satan a freer hand in order to demonstrate to all of creation his deceit and wickedness. As the time of Jesus' return approaches, Satan will gain an increasing hold over the world. Political, social, economic, and moral conditions will decay, culminating in a period of time the Bible speaks of as "the great tribulation." Almost all Bible scholars believe that this is a seven-year period. Whatever the exact number of years, it will be a time when Satan will gain near mastery of the world through a man totally controlled by him. This man will be a great world leader, thought to be a man of peace but who will ultimately bring to the world unprecedented persecution. Economic, social, and political organization as we know it today will all but disappear. War and famine and persecution will be worldwide and will affect everyone. The world will be in a state of chaos and life as it is today will be but a memory.

Such will be the state of the world at the time of Jesus' return. In drawing these conclusions from my reading and study, I had to admit some discomfort. It did not sound pleasant. Yet the end would see a victory for God and His people.

Somewhere in the midst of these events (the scholars disagree but most seem to place it either just before or during "the great tribulation"), an event of singular importance for the Christian is to take place. Historically it has been called "the rapture" and is the moment when God will snatch the Christians from the face of the earth in a moment to meet Him in heaven. This is the one aspect of the prophetic picture which has fascinated Christians and writers more than any other. It is the rapture that God will use to preserve His people to protect them from the wrath He will pour out on the earth. Christians will be raptured away from the earth just prior to the most intense time of suffering.

Naturally this delighted me.

When slowly it all began to come into focus, my outlook on many things began to change. Anticipating the future became entirely different. Telling people about the Lord and what is in store for the world became urgent; if they aren't "ready" they will miss the rapture.

So it remained for the next several years. I studied the Bible and was eager to learn all I could. What better way, I thought, to prepare for the future than to learn all I could in order to be more aware of what was going to happen?

Just as the girl I had overheard in the dinner line at Arrowhead Springs had said, a lot of things in my life—particularly my attitudes toward the future—did change as a result of Hal Lindsay's talk.

2

Prophecy Begins Hitting Closer to Home

Birth Pangs?

Years passed. College was soon behind me and my life

was filled with new responsibilities. I had a wife and family to provide for and a business to run. My interest in the future was forced to take a back seat to more practical and urgent matters. As the years slipped by, my initial excitement over Lindsay's talk faded into memory. I gradually thought less and less about the future. With bills to pay, children to raise, dishes to wash, leaks to fix, and bookstore fixtures to build, it was difficult to spend a lot of time wondering whether amillennialism or premillennialism was the proper interpretation of eschatology.

But in the mid-1970's all America was forced to take a long look at events taking place in the world. Several of these events had economic factors. Inflation was increasing phenomonally—something that affected us all. In many areas there were shortages which heightened the problem—gasoline, energy, water, foods. A visit to the grocery store gave dramatic evidence for the California drought, the eastern floods and the midwestern dust storms. Sitting alongside the gas pump at the service station made you immediately aware of the mid-Eastern oil embargos. The news each evening added to the list of world problems: disasters, shortages, wars, oil spills, explosions, bomb threats, hijackings, and price increases—all crises which eventually would find their way into our homes one way or another.

But the problems have not been purely economic. Watergate brought scandal and corruption right into our living rooms. The Nixon administration had lied to us. And as we read about the events later with some dawning historical perspective, it began to appear that the Democratic Congress and press had succeeded in ousting the wrongdoers from office in ways occasionally reminiscent of a lynch mob. By the time the Korean bribery scandal hit the papers we were so accustomed to corruption and immorality in high office that we hardly took notice. Corruption in government, from every side of the political spectrum, has become commonplace.

Many other factors have forced us to take notice of the condition of the world. We cannot help but be shocked. Rampant drug use—we have heard of nine-year-old and four-year-old addicts. Children have become the object of a billion-dollar porno industry. The public schools are often the breeding ground for crime. Programs that were once designed by the government to help those in need—welfare, unemployment, social security—have become a farce. On CBS's Sixty Minutes we see weekly examples of fraud, corruption, unfairness, violence, and law-breaking. We read that certain presidential candidates have paid no income tax while we shell out several thousand dollars. It seems that the equity, the stability, the justice in the world are gone.

Jimmy Carter was elected President and we hoped that as a Christian he would be able to help in some of these areas. But deep down I think most of us knew there was a limit to what he was going to be able to do. In our honest moments most of us would have to admit that it looks as though the world is on a collision course with disaster.

A growing awareness of the world situation brought these things into focus for me, and it all began to have a very familiar ring. I was reminded of Lindsay's talk and my earlier reading. "Wars and rumors of wars, famines, earthquakes . . . "—birth pangs.

"Hadn't Lindsay said they would grow more and more frequent and intense?"

As difficult as all these new current world developments have been to deal with on a daily level, they have served to remind me vividly about the times spoken of in the Bible as "the last days." Once again it begins to seem all the more likely to me that we are indeed living in that very time. I am once more paying close attention in light of the Bible prophecies to what is going on in the world.

During my awakening, however, there was one major thing that puzzled me as I looked around and witnessed all these unpleasant circumstances pressing ever closer. I had earlier assumed that the calamitous events of the world would not involve Christians. Most prophetic writers I was familiar with taught that we would be raptured away prior to such times. So I blithely assumed that somehow Christians would be spared from *all* forms of coming hardship and persecution. Shouldn't prophetic truth be joyful? Jesus is coming back! We will be caught up to meet Him!

I had emphasized but part of the truth. I had idealized it.

Youthful idealism is nothing new. When I was in college I idealized many things about my faith. Older men said things to me which I hardly heard. I thought I could merely say, "Trust in the Lord," and everything would be taken care of. Youth is a wonderful thing, but wisdom comes from years.

Now with a family and a business and large responsibilities, I found myself thinking about how to provide, protect, and maintain security—things I would have shunned as "carnal" earlier. "The world is coming apart," I thought, "and I have a responsibility to do what I can to shield my family from the effect of it."

So it was difficult for me to inject my earlier joyful idealism about prophecy into the current world scene—a scene hardly joyful. Christians were suffering as well. My prophetic eyes had for so long been turned toward the clouds, toward all the things that would happen far off in Israel—the building of the Temple, the ten-nation confederacy, the 144,000, the Battle of Armageddon, the two Witnesses—that I had failed to see that the inevitable collapse of world systems was bound to, at some point in its escalation, affect my family, my business, and those about me—Christians and non-Christians alike.

Unpleasant Forebodings

There have been hints of it for years, of course. Writers like Richard Wurmbrand and Aleksandr Solzhenitsyn have warned us that a new and different day is coming to the west; and that Christians had better prepare for it. It will be a day when it will not be easy to be a Christian. It will be a day when many of our present freedoms will be gone.

It is easy to overlook their predictions because they have not yet touched us personally with much force. Besides, these ideas give our favorite subject of prophecy such a nasty and gloomy feel. It isn't fun to think of persecution and hardship and deprivation and famine. Occasionally one will quote statistics about current events to prove that these truly are the last days and that Jesus is coming back soon. But when it comes down to deprivation and shortages and affliction in our own town, in our own home, we try to ignore the warnings of such men.

But the situation in the world presses in on us closer and closer. Prices continue to rise, various foods become increasingly scarce, terrorism and lawlessness seem to be everywhere. The "birth pangs" are getting closer; it is impossible to ignore them. Earlier when listening to Lindsay and when reading prophetic books, it had all sounded so exciting. Now, however, it has frightening aspects to it.

Let's take a look at David Wilkerson's *Vision.* [3]

"Persecution and tribulation and famine and suffering and deprivation and sin and lawlessness are coming *to us!*" cried Wilkerson. "Those things we read about in Revelation are not reserved for some *other* people in some *other* time. They're already happening in much of the world, and it's coming to us as well. It's no good thinking God is just going to whisk us away one of these days so we won't have to endure it. We have to face it, and prepare for it!"

I found this very discomforting when I first read it.

I began to realize that whether or not I as a Christian would actually go through the great tribulation isn't the only question. If Wilkerson is correct, then I am certain to be affected by the growing lawlessness, sin, rebellion, famine, and hardship throughout the world—whether it is the great tribulation spoken of in the Bible or simply a time of preparatory tribulation. The effect on my life will be great in either case.

I could no longer idealize prophecy, I concluded, interpreting world events theoretically. Rather than keeping it all "out there" where it failed to touch me personally, I knew the tribulation which was already coming upon the world would continue to deeply involve many aspects of my own life.

As a result of this awareness, my reading and thinking

have taken a new turn. I realize that in the face of current world circumstances, I cannot sit idly by watching all these things happen and simply wait for the Lord's return. Problems I face daily demand more of me than that. Even non-Christians are taking notice of the changing world scene and are preparing themselves as best they can to face it. Certainly as a Christian, recognizing the Lord's hand in everything about me, it becomes my responsibility to prepare for the days ahead as well.

Previously I felt my personal preparation to involve two things: study and evangelism. It was my responsibility to read books, scrutinize the prophetic sections of my Bible and study everything I could so as to most accurately understand what was going to happen. This was the first aspect of my preparation—gaining as much insight into biblical prophecy as possible. The second was to tell people about it so they would "be ready" as well. For me, *being ready* meant having certain knowledge and understanding.

I wonder, however, if my earlier "preparation through learning" was really preparation at all. Is that the sort of thing that will adequately equip me and my family for what we are bound to face in the coming years—even higher prices, more shortages, worse crime, run-away inflation, real hunger, actual persecution, etc.? All my "head knowledge" would be rather meager fare if my children were hungry and I had no food.

Naturally I know God will provide for us. My faith in God's provision has not diminished. Yet back then I could not help but wonder if there isn't something God expects me to do; something which, while trusting Him, nevertheless diligently prepares my family for what I am more and more certain lies ahead.

I was quite sure this didn't mean digging a huge underground shelter and storing up supplies. But I didn't know exactly what it did mean, either. In the days ahead, did God expect me to be as the lilies of the field who "neither toil or spin," or did He expect me to be as the man to whom His master gave a number of talents to multiply by using all his wisdom and diligence? Was I to sit back, "trusting

God" to supply all my need? Or was I, still trusting God, to strike out aggressively to arm myself for providing for my family and those about me?

To discover answers to these questions I have found myself once again delving into a study of biblical prophecy, though this time it has been from a different angle with a host of new questions.

Two Purposes of God in Our Future

My reading took me in two directions I had not foreseen. It had previously been easy to think of the persecution coming in the world as sort of a "necessary evil"—something almost out of God's hands, certainly known by Him but not originating with Him.

But now I wasn't so sure.

I began to see that through this persecution and hardship, God had a magnificent purpose in mind for His people. When Jesus returns to earth it not only is to defeat the forces of Satan but also to claim His bride, His body—God's people. And the Bible tells us that when He does come for His bride, the Church, it will be "without spot or blemish." God's people will be united—one. God means to purify and cleanse His people.

This really is not so new. We have always known this. But what made me begin to stand up and take notice were the numerous scriptures I encountered which clearly teach that such purification can only come about by fire. Through discipline, tribulation and hardship are God's people made perfect. There is no other way (Malachi 3:3; 4:1-2; Mark 9:49; Romans 5:3-4, 1 Corinthians 3:13; Hebrews 5:8-9). God, therefore, intends to purify His people and make them "one" largely through the tribulation they will face prior to Jesus' return.

But there is a second purpose in this purification process. In addition to preparing us for Jesus' coming, the Church is to minister to the world in the midst of its tribulation. As never before the Church will be "the light of the world." In many ways God's people will provide the stabilizing force that will help bind the people of the world together.

These two aspects of God's work in us and through us go hand in hand. The more God's people minister to those about them, the more Satan will insure that they are even more heavily persecuted. Because God's people are the strongest threat to the purposes of Satan, he will do everything in his power to destroy them.

Realizing these purposes of God for me and for other Christians in the coming years revealed to me the shortsightedness of my earlier expectation that I would be raptured away prior to the time of extreme stress and hardship. Though I did not know exactly when the rapture fit into God's plan, this had become ever more clear—*God has a people to purify and a world to heal*. Persecution and deprivation are in many ways the key to the purification, and a united church is the key to the healing. Christians are certain to face many of these things in order that God's purpose for us be fulfilled.

3

The Key to a Christian's Preparation— Separation From the World

Two Tribulations Are Coming

Though I now see that hardship is an integral part of God's purpose for me in the future, I have not sat down and invited hardship to come upon me. Though Jesus knew the cross was at the end of His earthly road, He did not immediately go from Nazareth to Jerusalem to be offered. In fact, He frequently slipped away from the authorities who would have killed Him sooner if they could. Jesus was not trying to avoid God's purpose for Him. But He knew something of God's timing. He knew it was not God's design for Him to foolishly walk into the hands of His enemies before the time was right.

So as I read the Proverbs ("the industrious man reaps a

rich harvest"—12:27; "victory is the fruit of long planning"—11:14; "diligence brings a man to power"—12:24, NEB), and as I considered the responsibility God has given me as a husband and a father, I perceive my task toward my family to be twofold. First, knowing that tribulation is coming upon the world and that God intends to purify Christians through it, to act as a "spiritual head" over my family so that God is able to do His complete work in each one of them. And secondly, to protect and shield my family from the negative effects of the coming hardship and persecution as long as God gives me the capability to do so.

There is both a positive and negative thrust to the things that are coming upon the world—Satan's attempt to destroy and God's plan to purify and heal. We must protect ourselves from the one while submitting ourselves to the other.

As we mentioned before, Jesus himself faced the question of when to submit to the evil about Him and when to escape it. I wondered, "How much should I try to safeguard my family from the evil that is coming, and how much should I allow those difficulties to have an internal chastening effect on us?" As the head of my family, ever on my mind was the question, "How can I most effectively shield them from Satan's influence through the sin and tribulation in the world, and yet keep them secure but 'growing through suffering' in God's love and blessing?"

To find the balance between the two, I took my cue from two scriptures. The first is 2 Samuel 24:14, in which David chose his punishment for wrongdoing from the hand of the Lord rather than from men; and the second, John 18:11, in which Jesus at His arrest said, "This is the cup the Father has given me to . . . drink." In both cases, the persecution that followed came straight from God. Many times both David and Jesus did their utmost to escape punishment and evil that men would have inflicted upon them. But when it came from God, they willingly submitted.

Therefore I began to sense my duty to be willing to submit to any purifying hardship *the Lord* chooses to send upon me, but otherwise to make every effort to escape from and shield my family from the effects of tribulation and evil and hardships which have become increasingly prevalent throughout the world at the hand of Satan.

In addition to ministering to my family, how can I prepare myself to most effectively minister to those about me in the coming days and years? I have a responsibility to other Christians as well as to non-Christians who suffer in the world.

It seems the answer to both desires (defending my family against the hardships caused by Satan and acquiring the means and capacity to minister to those around me) lies in somehow lessening my dependence on the world and its systems. The more independent we become from the world's crumbling economy, the more God will be able to take care of all our needs in spite of what is going on in the world.

Jesus has always made it clear that we are to be "in" the world but not "of" the world. Now more than ever I see the urgent need for Christians to become set apart from the world in as many ways as possible—not simply concerning spiritual things but also financially and economically and physically. The less we are dependent on the institutions of the world, the less severe will be the effects of the increasing hardships on us; and the more, therefore, we will be in positions to minister to those for whom the effects have been severe.

Throughout my thinking and study, I kept wondering in the back of my mind, "Are these *really* the end times?" I looked at the 80¢ a gallon for gas, 80¢ for a loaf of bread, and $50,000 for an average home as irritating but hardly spiritually significant things.

"It's just inflation," I would sigh; "I don't like it, but does it really signal the beginning of what Lindsay called 'the countdown'?"

But when I added to inflation everything else I was witnessing daily—corruption, anarchy, the oil shortage, the energy crisis, population and pollution and food problems, starvation in Africa and China and India, the constant wars in the Middle East, Africa, and Southeast Asia, the worldwide nuclear threats, the soaring crime rates, and failing economies, I felt I had no choice but to conclude, "Yes, these are the times Jesus spoke of. Lindsay, Wilkerson, and the Bible prophets all warned of this. The time is at least close at hand."

As I read Wurmbrand, Popov, Kordakov, Brother Andrew, and others about life as a Christian behind the Iron Curtain, I cannot ignore the realization that one day, possibly very soon, such conditions could be upon us here in the free west.

Dependence on the World's Systems

I know, of course, that neither I nor anyone else can ever be fully prepared for what lies ahead. Yet I feel that to be no reason to neglect what preparation is possible. The more the world falls apart, the more additional aspects of our lives will be directly held in God's hands. And throughout the process I want to use the facilities and abilities He has given me for the utmost good. I want to be a diligent follower, capable of using even a little that God gave me for the greatest possible benefit to others.

I have this growing assurance that foresight, planning, and training are a definite part of God's work in my life for future preparedness.

Daily, it seems, the world grows further from the principles of God. I recognize that unless at some point I take a stand to separate myself from that drift which is occurring, I will be in danger of being gradually ensnared by it. The changes come about so slowly that it is relatively easy to float along with the world for a time. But the snare grips us tighter all the time until escape is almost impossible.

Over a period of time, my emphasis and my goal have become "How can I set myself apart from the world? How can I lessen my dependence on it? How can I provide for my family and increase my methods of ministry to others in ways independent of the world?"

I know it is easy to say, "I depend on the Lord for everything." But if my paycheck comes from the U.S. Government, Georgia-Pacific, the School Board, or Acme Corporation; and if I buy my food at Safeway or the A & P, and my clothes at Sears or Penney's and drive a Chevrolet; and if my children go to public school, it is clear that much of my life will be tightly bound up in institutions of the world.

Of course it is essential to trust the Lord internally concerning spiritual matters even though these other things may be a part of our external lives. And certainly the Lord is easily able to work through these institutions to accomplish His will. Nevertheless, these institutions do remain "middle men." So it becomes my increasing desire to answer the question, "How can I lessen my dependence on these middle men?" Is it possible?

It is not that General Motors or Sears are intrinsically evil and that we shouldn't work for them or buy their products. That is not the point at all. The point is simply this: we must realize where the world is headed. It is going downhill and many of these institutions will be going down with it. If our lives are rigidly bound to them, we will one day find ourselves pulled down as well.

For years my admittedly selfish ambition has been to get a small plot of land somewhere out in the country where my family and I could live a quiet and peaceful life, providing for ourselves completely. And such a vision is tempting because it so neatly answers the question, "How can I provide for my family in the face of coming hardship and persecution?"

But it is an idealized solution. I imagine I could accomplish such a thing eventually if I made it a key priority of life. But then what of my responsibility to the rest of my family, God's body? What of my responsibility to minister to others in need?

The fact is, it is just about impossible in today's world for the average person to "go it alone." For the Christian especially, God's purpose in the days ahead is not to completely remove us from the world so that we cease to be involved with those around us. We will never be able to divorce ourselves entirely from society; we should not want to because our ministry to it would be ended. But we can begin right where we presently are discovering ways to prepare for the future. The small efforts we make now to separate ourselves from the world will have a multiplying effect over the years, since the gap between the world and the principles of God is growing ever wider.

One of the key factors in my being able both to separate myself from the world and minister to those in it involves my relationship with my fellow Christians. As the world's economy continues in upheaval, I will increasingly be forced to depend on other Christians for a wider variety of goods and services if I plan not to depend on the institutions of the world. The time may well come when Christians will not be permitted to buy or sell in secular stores. Christians will have to provide for each other. We will have to live and function as a community in the midst of a world we have little interaction with. Our food will have to be supplied by other Christians. We will call upon our brothers for services of all kinds. And they will call upon us as well to provide what we have—food, gifts, tools, talents, money, abilities and special skills. There will have to be an increased sharing and interdependence.

In preparation for that time, we must begin to function that way as much as possible now.

Not only will our survival be dependent on the degree to which we as Christians come together and function as a single body, but this style of life will also be the way God enables us to minister to those non-Christians who have needs. Because of the free flow between God's people, there will be an abundance God will be able to use to help those outside the Body.

This giving and receiving and living in harmony—providing for one another and ministering to others—will have a large share in what God will use to spiritually ready His people for the return of Jesus. He will make us one body through these times of testing and trial when we learn to live and love and serve together.

A further means of readying ourselves for the future, and which only indirectly involves a separation from the world, has to do with what we might term "survival training." Many things fall in this category—eating, cooking, exercising, acquiring skills, earning money on our own, gardening, etc. Separating ourselves from the world is an all-inclusive task which eventually will affect every area of life.

The more I have thought about all these aspects of the future and their influence on my life and my family's, the more diverse become the areas I have tried to incorporate into my preparatory measures. As a well-known saying goes, spiritually speaking "the future is as bright as the promises of God." But physically, as we contemplate the years ahead, the future is not bright. Though God is going to do great things in our hearts through it, yet nevertheless we must soberly realize that much of our preparation is just this—survival training. We will experience deprivation like never before. The more equipped we are to deal with it, on every level, the less it will negatively influence our capacity to love and serve God.

You have now come with me briefly through the thought processes in which God has led as a result of my reading and study over the past ten years. Now I will share with you how I am learning to cut off my dependence on the world, training myself to survive as a man of God when more intense deprivation comes.

Part II
PREPARING FOR THE FUTURE
WITH OUR HANDS

Looking at my own life to determine those areas where I could begin to cut myself off from an utter dependence on the world as well as train myself both to survive and minister as deprivation in the world increased, one area began to stand out. I saw that I was going to have to gain proficiency with my hands in a wide variety of ways.

At first my response was, "Isn't it rather mundane to associate my physical expertise in some area with the high and weighty matters of spiritual prophecy? After all, how could my ability to fix a leak or build an addition on my home possibly have anything to do with the return of Jesus?"

As I considered the matter in more depth, however, several things began to stand out. It became clear that, practically speaking, the more Christians actually were separated from the world the more they would have to "fend for themselves." A skilled professional won't necessarily always be just a phone call away. We will often have to do what needs to be done ourselves. In cases where I had no previous knowledge for a certain task I would have to rely on my brother Christians. And there would be times they would come to me for help as well.

As difficult as it was for me to try to incorporate such

down-to-earth matters into my earlier study and "prophetic knowledge," it began to look very practical indeed as I anticipated the future—practical not only in the sense of getting things done, but also as it would begin to bring about a community life-style of harmony and working together between Christians. I could see there would be many, many opportunities to share and exchange skills and abilities to meet various needs that will arise. We will want to freely share what God has given us.

The element of ministry should be considered as well. People of all kinds, Christians and non-Christians alike, are going to find themselves facing a multitude of needs in the days ahead, many of them physical. The more equipped I can become, therefore, to help with those needs—be they spiritual or simple everyday tasks—the more opportunities I will have to share the love of Jesus with those who are unaware of the significance of the times we are living in.

And from the standpoint of thrift and prudence, particularly as money becomes more scarce, I see the advantage of my learning to do as much for myself as possible. In the coming years I know I will rarely be able to afford the luxury of having someone else do work for me that I am physically capable of doing. As a responsible father and husband I have no other choice but to learn to work effectively with my hands.

In addition to these purely practical and economic factors, I began to see as well that my ability to work and accomplish things with my hands is a demonstration of God's creativity, love and imagination. He created these bodies of ours to work, and to work hard. "You shall gain your bread by the sweat of your brow" (Gen. 3:19). In today's sedentary society many jobs do not require strenuous physical output. My own job is ordinarily like that: demanding, yes; physically backbreaking, no. If I take this injunction seriously, I have to rely on regular exercise and industriousness during my leisure hours to make me "sweat."

I do not feel there is a great deal of merit, however, in sweating simply for hard work's sake (digging a hole merely to fill it back in again). God is a God of wisdom, planning, accomplishment, vision, and imagination. His ways are purposeful. Besides giving us physical strength and nimble hands, God also has conferred upon us wisdom and a little of His own creativity. No matter what the task, I should be able to observe in it a degree of achievement and something of the character of God. This was a new insight to me in my early study, and added a certain zest to my work. It became a joy to make or fix things and to work creatively with my hands and imagination, knowing that God was being reflected in my work. It was just as true when cleaning a bathroom or weeding a lawn as when constructing a unique piece of fine furniture. If my heart attitude was aware of it, such labor gave glory to God.

Edith Schaeffer describes this latent creativity in us all which God is waiting to develop as "left-over" bits of the creativity with which God first fashioned the world. She says, "There is . . . beauty in the creation of God. Since He created man as a creative creature, by creating him in His own image . . . [man has] through the ages retained fragments of the perfection which He made in the first place." She goes on to add, "The Christian should have more vividly expressed creativity in his daily life, and have more creative freedom, as well as the possibility of a continuing development in creative activities." [4]

To Mrs. Schaeffer this creativity of God can and should be expressed in our lives through a diversity of outlets—musical expression, hobbies, gardening, arranging flowers, repairing furniture, painting, decorating, preparing meals, and recreation. No area of life is insignificant. Such expression is possible because we have been made in the image of God; the total scope of our lives is involved, not just those areas we may think of as specifically artistic.

To me, with little mechanical aptitude, watching a friend take the engine out of a car, overhaul it, and then put it back in once again is to witness a highly ingenious virtuoso performance. I am similarly awed to observe the work of a skilled cabinet maker, a proficient seamstress, or an experienced stone mason. Such people are artists, in my estimation. They are allowing the creativity and expression of

God inside them to flow from their minds and out through their hands into the things they make and do. Many of you are familiar with Joni Eareckson, a quadriplegic who has glorified God enormously with her beautiful pen "mouth drawings" and accompanying testimony. What an assertion of God's imagination!

The same can be said about any of us and anything we do when we allow God to work through and develop the gifts He has given us. It need not have an acclaimed and magnificent result. Fixing a leak under the bathroom sink can give God glory whenever we use it as an opportunity to thank Him and express His goodness.

There are, therefore, two good reasons why competence with our hands is important: it is highly practical and necessary, as well as deeply spiritual, when creativity is able to work into our spirits. Acquiring physical skills must be a salient part of a Christian's dedicated preparation for the future.

1

Being a Handyman

Create With Your Hands

As attaining a certain degree of competence in various areas began to become more important to me, I looked ahead with an expanding set of priorities regarding ways I could prepare for the future as a Christian. I looked at my own life with the realization that there were few things I was able to do with my hands. When I was married I knew how to do practically nothing. Though my father was handy with his hands, somehow it never seemed to rub off on me. Being married, however, as well as owning a store and a home, forced me to learn to accomplish many things myself. We didn't have the money to call a plumber for every leak and a carpenter for every small repair or remodeling job. So I learned to do what I could.

The first major project I tackled was to make new fixtures for our bookstore. We were growing and expanding and needed a new shelf to display our Bibles. Up to that point we had managed to skimp by on racks I had bought, shelves others made for me, and the fixtures I had inherited when taking over the store. I had never yet made anything from scratch. But this time I knew I would never find just what I wanted second or third hand. If I wanted the shelves, they would have to be my own doing.

The first step was to sit down and draw some sketches of what I wanted. I worked hard on the drawings, making changes here and there, analyzing the store's needs, the space we had available for the shelves, and what exactly I wanted them to hold. Finally I came up with a completed picture. I figured out exactly how much wood to buy and carted it to a friend's home (I had no tools of my own); with the various stacks of wood all laid out before me, I proceeded with the first few cuts I was sure about. I had to ask my friend for advice and help about every five minutes at first, but over the next several days the procedure became more and more familiar until I was making decisions with amazing confidence! After several weeks the three shelves began to take form and were completed. And they looked good!

I was excited. I had actually *made* something from start to finish. There was a definite thrill and fulfillment to the accomplishment.

This was only the beginning. It showed me that it is possible for anyone to work with his hands—to build, to fix, to create. My assumption had been that you had to have some special knack for it. But the Bible shelves standing before me demonstrated just the opposite.

I thought, "I can build other shelves we need." And I did. Over the next several years I made dozens of bookshelves. When five years later we opened a second store, nearly every fixture originated in my garage shop. Granted, I am still far from a professional. If an expert saw some of my handywork he might cringe! Nevertheless, the fixtures are functional, and in addition we have probably saved several thousand dollars in labor costs at the store through remodeling and maintenance work I have done myself. Again, some of it is undoubtedly crude work. But gradually I've learned to do the things we've needed to have done.

My point is precisely this: we needn't all be professional artisans in order to express God's creativity with our hands. My wife and I have found ourselves learning to do many new things in our home as well, from planting a garden to painting and paneling our living room to converting a spare bedroom into a library. Little things? Certainly. Yet years earlier they would have seemed like insurmountably difficult tasks. Gradually we have gained the confidence to undertake larger projects. We have experimented with minor plumbing leaks, painted our house, put on a new roof, added a baby room in the attic, laid bricks to install a Franklin fireplace, insulated our ceiling. . . .

There's no doubt many men can still do more with their hands than I can. My skills are minimal. Learning to work with my hands has thrilled me nevertheless because I see two things at work. For one thing there is a new element in my relationship with God. I am more aware of His creativity and imagination. We *can* bring into reality visions He gives us. And in addition I know these attempts of mine are providing vital practice for the days that lie ahead.

I can no longer content myself with a compartmentalization of my responsibility to God, thinking that only traditionally "spiritual" things matter. It will be necessary that I be able to meet all sorts of needs. This means a capability of mind, emotions, spirit, hands, skills, resources, and talents all woven together. God will need a *total* people.

Anyone Can Learn Right Where He Is

Knowing this, how can we learn to do things with our hands? How do we become handymen?

The first step is to do the basic maintenance on our homes as much as possible—fix leaks, repair breaks, remodel rooms, landscape yards, control weeds, and so on. We have to become an apprentice all-around-fix-it man. Some Christians may find it difficult to see the spiritual necessity of a nicely painted home, a well-landscaped yard with green lawn, and a home free of the need for obvious repair. "Why bother with these temporal things? Jesus might be coming back soon."

I have fallen into this line of thinking myself whenever I forget that my life is a total unit. Faithfulness, orderliness and diligence must touch every aspect of life. These are part of our total stewardship to God. As one of His people, I am aware that it is my obedient responsibility to be a witness to the truth to the world. An unkempt life in need of external repair reflects internal traits as well. The inward transformation that has taken place in our hearts as a result of God's love should naturally find expression in our care for our environment.

Acquiring manual proficiencies is not only the man's responsibility. Proverbs 31 portrays a godly handywoman who is well able to provide many things for those in her family. Daily cooking and sewing, often taken for granted by the rest of the household, require a good deal of time and training and provide many opportunities for the creative woman. Though they can be tedious, such tasks take on special meaning for the woman who views them as occasions for expressing the love of God. There are all sorts of things a woman can do to add to the attractiveness and functionality of her home—make curtains, design a cupboard for her husband to make, cover an old chair, find bargains on used furniture. . . . In our first home my wife made our window curtains from sheets and stitched together a patchwork carpet from samples we picked up free from local stores. She has painted our bedroom and dressers, makes most of our boys' clothes and many of my own. We know another mother who is a skilled carpenter. She has completely re-done rooms, made bunk beds for her children as well as painted several nice oil paintings for their home.

Naturally, everyone won't be gifted in the same areas. And wonderful results are not accomplished overnight. But every one of us can learn to master things which may presently be totally foreign to us, if we are willing to practice. We must begin to explore the areas of interest we do have in order to make a beginning.

How do you start? You simply dig in right where you are

with whatever opportunities present themselves.

One holiday my wife and I had looked forward to with special anticipation because it fell on our anniversary. But early that morning we spotted a leak under the bathroom sink. I decided I would try to fix it myself; and, unfortunately, by the time the drip was finally stopped, our day together was practically gone. I had begun by taking apart the joint and finding a worn piece. Then I went to the hardware store (taking the worn-out piece), talked to a clerk (who knew *much* more about it than I did). He told me how to install the new part, and I returned home already more knowledgeable than before. (Ask questions! Most people are glad to tell you what they know. I think 50% of what I've learned about things has been from asking questions and listening carefully to the answers—the other 50% has come from practice.)

It took three or four hours (frustrating hours!) to install the new joint and to stop all the resultant leaks. It was not a particularly "fun" day—on my back with water dripping in my face. But I did learn a lot. Since then I have taken on tougher plumbing jobs (dishwasher leaks, broken garbage disposals)—some successfully, others not. We've had to call a plumber a few times. But had I not simply jumped in (with both feet *and* all my ignorance) and tried a few times, I would never have learned anything at all.

If you insist on waiting until you are able to do every job perfectly, you will get little practice. The little problems that creep into every project should be laughed at rather than despaired over. I built my wife a little wooden case to hold her music. I figured every cut slowly and deliberately, making certain each measurement was precise. I wanted it to be perfect. Somehow though, when I was all through, one of the shelves slanted noticeably downhill. It was too late to make a correction; it was there forever. (I still don't have the slightest idea what happened.)

It seems that every job I complete has elements like that—imperfections, uneven edges, mismatched joints, rough spots. But I don't stop work because of them. I know learning skills in this manner is good for me. My usefulness in God's family is slowly increasing all the time.

Many carpentry skills can be learned simply by embarking on a project. You don't need every elaborate tool; actually, you need very few. All it takes is a picture of what you want to make and the materials. From there you decide on what the first step needs to be, then the second, and so on. With such a plan before you, begin with step one and *do* it. Then go on to step two, then three. Before long your picture will have become a reality.

You can learn most anything in this manner.

Occasionally, however, more detailed instruction is necessary. For several years in our store we sold handcrafted leather Bible covers. When our source for these covers discontinued making them, I thought it would be good if we could make them ourselves so we could go on carrying them. But when I looked at the covers with all their intricate colors and designs, I knew they were works of art. "I'm not the least bit artistic," I thought. "I could never do that kind of work."

Nevertheless it seemed to be worth investigating to find out what was involved in making them. I asked a man I knew who had worked with leather for a couple of years if it would be possible to teach someone like me how to make a Bible cover, even though I'd had no prior experience. "Sure," he said; "there's nothing to it!"

And he proved to be right. After only a half hour's instruction I had learned what I needed to know to continue with it on my own. It was simply a matter of being shown the proper technique. After investing about $50 in tools, we were then able to carry on with the making and selling of Bible covers. I subsequently taught two more people the technique and now we do a greater volume in our little leather corner than we ever dreamed possible.

Naturally there are times when the in-depth instruction of a book, the advice of an expert, a class, or a period of apprenticeship is needed. But practice remains the key to learning skills.

A Diversity of Practical Capabilities

Being a handyman isn't necessarily limited to simple odd jobs. Though it may begin with relatively easy things that we can do with our hands, the implications for expanded physical and mental inventiveness are limitless. The all-around capable Christian who is not dependent on the world and other people wherever he turns demonstrates a deft resourcefulness throughout many aspects of his life.

For example, my wife does all the accounting for our business. She has had no formal training for it but has learned by doing. Our business has grown rapidly and there have been difficult periods when the figures, taxes, quarterly reports, and profit and loss statements have so confused us we became overwhelmed by it all. At such times we have had to go to professional accountants to get help through these transitional stages. But on the whole she has managed it alone and it has saved us many thousands of dollars in accountant fees.

In a similar manner, when our business grew increasingly complex and we saw the need to incorporate, I decided I would work at drawing up the incorporation papers rather than paying a lawyer $1000 to do it. So I wrote letters, talked to people, and found out details about the procedure. It was not easy. I did make mistakes, had to refile several of the applications, and had to have an attorney's help at one point in the process to bail us out of a minor problem my ignorance had caused. It turned out to be a six-month affair, whereas it would have taken a lawyer but a month or two. But eventually it got done and was entirely legal. Besides the valuable experience I gained, we did save the money.

Does this begin to make sense to you?

This "self-sufficiency" I advocate isn't meant to cause us to ignore everyone about us and the Lord as well. What I am trying to teach myself is to acquire practical skills that give God glory now, increase the ways I am able to care for my family, and will keep us from being at the mercy of the non-Christian world in times to come. And I want to be available to help my Christian brothers when they have needs as well, knowing of course that they will be there to help us also.

Every one of us cannot be highly proficient in every skill. God distributes talents very diversely among the body. With my limited mechanical aptitude, I simply do not understand the workings of a car. I hope someday to know more than I do now. But at present I must rely on my brothers who are gifted in that area. Certain things such as this I leave in knowledgeable and experienced hands. It would not be wise and could be dangerous for a beginner to undertake a complicated electrical job. Wisdom, care, and prayerfulness must accompany our diligent attempts to learn. If we set out to become a novice electrician, we need to be prudent and seek skilled help throughout the process.

2

Gardening

Here's an area where anyone can acquire the necessary skills; growing your own food certainly provides one of the most practical means of preparing for the future and for providing for our families in the meantime. Circumstances could well arise where we will be forced to "live off the land" again as our forefathers once did. Many factors we have already discussed can contribute to this: rampant price increases, food scarcity, famine, and economic and political collapse. Producing food efficiently will not be optional in the last days; it will be necessary for survival.

We can prepare for those times now by learning all we can about growing food and then putting into practice what we learn. Waiting until famine is upon us will be too late. We must already have had years of practice by then and a certain degree of proficiency.

Growing your own food is not only a preparatory measure, however. With prices escalating as never before, it is simply a good sound economic suggestion. Home-grown vegetables are more healthy (and more fun) to eat, and you can save money by growing them as well.

My wife and I are not green-thumb gardeners. What we have learned has been from reading, talking to people, and practice.

We have had a garden now for four years. Two years ago we had enough spinach to eat some every week or two for most of the winter. Our carrots, however, were a dismal failure. Last year, thinking to balance things out somewhat, we planted more carrots. The resulting crop of carrots overflowed our freezer; the majority of our spinach plants, however, went to seed shortly after coming up. We barely had enough for a couple of meals. This year it appears that potatoes are going to be the bumper crop.

Gardening is unpredictable, but fun nevertheless!

To *start* a garden you don't need to know much of anything. But as you progress, knowledge on various aspects of the process will become increasingly necessary. There are hundreds, probably thousands, of books written on every conceivable aspect of gardening. What is "organic"? How does one make compost? How about mulch gardening, earthworms, types of soils, affect of climate, diseases and insects, winter crops, fertilizers? When should one harvest, etc.? If you intend to have a healthy, producing garden, you will need to spend some time reading. The growing is but the beginning. From there you must learn how to use the food most efficiently. Such kitchen subjects are a whole new world in themselves—canning, freezing, baking, preparing, storing, drying—and offer one of the most significant ways a woman can ready herself for the strenuous years ahead. Your garden and your kitchen are areas of stewardship. Work in them as unto the Lord.

Fruit trees are exciting as well. No matter whether you're working with a tiny yard or several acres, you can grow some of your own fruit. Your selection will depend on climate, of course. Apples, pears, plums, and cherries do well most anyplace. Citrus fruits, peaches, apricots, and so on, require considerable sunshine.

Climate is a factor in all aspects of your gardening venture that will largely determine what you can grow and when you can plant. Talk to people whose gardens are a success year after year. Experiment with different methods. Read. Your success will be built on the foundation you invest in it.

Berries, both domestic and wild, are a joy to grow or find. What a thrill to discover a virgin patch of ripe blackberries! Once you begin to see all the things you can pick or grow or glean from the earth itself, from God's hand, going to the store to buy them pales in comparison.

God made us to interact with His living and growing creation. We are a part of that creation. Fruits, nuts, vegetables, grains, berries, and herbs were given us by God and are expressions of His love. Think for a moment of the enormous variety found in the thousands of foods God made. Imagine the colors, sizes, tastes, textures. Consider the different places of the world where different foods are found. Remember the ways foods grow: in shells, underground, on trees, on vines, as roots. What a joy it must have been for God to create all these things *for us*!

Every juicy fruit we bite into is genuinely God's special gift to us. Growing our own foods then makes us partakers in a divine and centuries-old process. There is something fulfilling to our spirits about the close interaction with God's earth.

Many of the truths in God's Word are shared with us by means of illustrations concerning growing, gardening, watering, planting, bearing fruit, etc.:

"I am the vine, you are the branches. . . . "

" . . . he it is that bears much fruit."

"Except a grain of wheat fall into the ground. . . . "

"A sower went out to sow."

"My Father is the vinedresser. . . . "

" . . . every branch that does not bear fruit he prunes, that it may bear more fruit."

"I planted, Apollos watered, but God gave the growth."

" . . . other seeds fell into good soil and brought forth grain."

" . . . and seeing a fig tree he found no fruit on it."

On nearly every page it seems there are such references—soil, seeds, weeds, fruit, vines, figs, soil, growth. We will be able to gain the most complete understanding of the truths of the Bible when we are familiar with the growth process firsthand. Growing living things is a thrilling way to make the truths of God's word *live*.

Part III

PREPARING OUR BODIES FOR THE FUTURE

As I read books about the future as well as about the current conditions in much of the world, it is plain that the level of comfort and ease which make up our style of life in this country at present can not go on forever. This is a growing awareness to a host of experts whose predictions are purely social and economic and have nothing whatever to do with events as the Bible foretells them. Looking ahead with the growing sense that God's people are to be anticipating the return of Jesus and therefore making themselves ready for the strenuous days the Bible indicates will precede His coming, I have realized that the stresses of those times will be felt initially in the physical world.

If the world systems continued to plunge toward eventual ruin, the coming years will become increasingly characterized by many sorts of deprivation. The Great Depression has served as a reminder. Then everything was scarce; there simply wasn't enough to go around. And many economic authorities predict such times are coming again soon—food shortages and famine in many parts of the world, intensifying oil and energy crises augmented by a population growth rate out of control in many areas, as well as widespread wars and revolutions erupting all over the globe as a result of these conditions.

For millions now living in underprivileged countries where starvation is already commonplace, such times will hardly signal a drastic shift. But for those of us living in relative wealth and luxury, such a transition will be immense. There will be much we will quickly have to learn to do without. Those things that affect us physically—food, clothing, shelter, and so on—will be the hardest hit, and they will also cause the most difficult adjustments. Being hungry day in and day out is a feeling already known by millions who are comparatively used to it. Those of us, however, who regularly have more than we possibly need will find going hungry a new and unpleasant experience.

Our stomachs will be only one place we feel the effects. When crisis and inflation undermine the economy to the extent that many highly skilled men find themselves without jobs, it will be difficult to get used to working with their hands to scratch out a living for their families. Satan will use these times. He knows how difficult physical hardship is for us. When accusing Job to God, he said, "You have always protected him and his home and his property from all harm. You have prospered everything he does—look how rich he is! No wonder he 'worships' you! But just take away his wealth, and you'll see him curse you to your face!" (Job 1:10-11, TLB). Will Satan try to use the same ploy in coming years to make Christians turn their backs on God? World conditions will undoubtedly provide him unlimited opportunities.

Physical preparation and fitness, therefore, are highly practical in light of what seems to lie ahead. But for the Christian it becomes a vital part of our stewardship to God as well. We must arm ourselves for the day when we may have to stand in our ancient brother Job's shoes and say when everything has been stripped from us, "The Lord gives and the Lord takes away; blessed be the name of the Lord!" (Job 1:21). But as God's children it is also our responsibility to take care of our bodies (as well as everything He gives us) and maintain them at the highest level possible. The body is one of God's most marvelous gifts to man. He expects us to sustain both body and spirit so that we will be both physically *and* spiritually capable to minister effectively. Wise stewardship of our bodies, considering the changes that are soon coming to the physical world around us, is faithful preparation for what we will face as children of God.

1
Wise Eating

Hardship Will Demand Physical Preparedness

Any attempt at diligent bodily stewardship, for whatever reason, must begin with a discussion of foods and eating habits—the fuel we provide our bodies.

When I first began to incorporate wider phases of my life into my provisions for the days ahead, I wondered, "How could my eating habits possibly have anything to do with the future, with biblical prophecy and current world events?"

But the more I considered my own potential role, the more correlation I could see between the deprivation I was sure was coming and my own physical and bodily readiness. I knew food could be in short supply; the abundance and variety we know today just wouldn't be available. I knew I could be forced to live on little food or only one type of available food for a long period of time. Therefore I began to realize that unless my body was in peak shape—my internal organs and digestive system functioning at maximum efficiency—such changes would be severe. Therefore, the only way for my body to be in top form to handle those situations forced upon it *then* would be to prepare and train it *now*. And I could see this would be accomplished only as I took care of my body daily—what I ate, how much I ate, what I drank, my exercise habits, my weight, my ailments, my sleeping habits, and so on. The usefulness and healthfulness of the food I was putting in my body, therefore, began to become a high priority in my thoughts. "If I am going to be an effective child of God in the coming years," I reasoned, "then my bodily mechanisms are going to have to be working at full strength and vigor."

Were famine to strike, if I had not had so much as a day of preparation, my body would not be prepared in the least for the diet I might face. There would be an initial shock as my body tried to cope with the change. My lack of readiness would produce physical inefficiency which could also lead to fatigue, apathy, depression, and a lack of trust in God.

Then my thoughts turned to persecution. I knew as a Christian I had to realistically face that it will eventually come, as it already has behind the Iron Curtain. What if one day I find myself in prison? The food there will certainly be skimpy and vastly unnourishing. Only if my body is in top form already will I be able to keep from getting sick and weak. It will be the most efficient body, the one whose digestion and circulation and elimination is working properly, that will most efficiently use the food it does get to sustain itself. The Christian whose body is in good working order will be most able to minister effectively to those around him.

Possibly, I thought, before either famine or prison, an economic boycott might be levied against those who refuse to openly acknowledge a political system or ruler whom we Christians know is not from God. Revelation 13:17 certainly prepares us for the reality of such an idea: "No one could get a job or even buy in any store without the permit of that mark . . ." (TLB).

And one thing is certain above all else: those days are going to require useful Christians—strong, ministering, joyful, effective Christians, unhampered by weakness of body, soul, or spirit!

In college when I ran many mile and half-mile races on many different tracks around the west, my body was in peak form and finely tuned. I ran for seven years without ever taking a "vacation" from training. If the slightest thing went wrong, I could feel it immediately as I ran. In looking toward the future I had the desire to regain an element of that "fine tuning." But this time I wanted it to include the entire scope of my being—physical, emotional, and spiritual—not simply that my body was well exercised and in condition. To come to the final days unprepared, I felt, would be comparable to my walking into a stadium completely out of shape and lining up for the mile finals in my street clothes.

Our Unknowing Abuse of God's Magnificent Creation

I began to think of my eating habits as a necessary aspect of my training, in much the same way as I had looked upon running up tall sand dunes while training for competitive running. I was awed by the magnificent machine my body is—especially when I thought about some of the "junk" I put into it each day. It is amazing that God seems to have created our bodies to be able to run on most anything. If you put water into a gasoline tank, a car won't so much as budge. If you merely alter the mixture of gas, you can tell the difference immediately.

Not so with our bodies!

We can stuff ourselves full of food having practically no nutritional content day after day, year after year, yet somehow our bodies continue to function fairly well. God put into us a great deal of inherent power—a lot of himself!

Yet I could tell this very wonder was the root of one of my most serious nutritional problems. Because our bodies are such amazing instruments, they rarely signal us immediately when we abuse them. If I feed my body something harmful, it usually manages to cope with my carelessness.

But even as my body so marvelously adapts itself, nevertheless in the long run it is affected by such treatment. Since reading about its internal workings (digestion, organs, elimination, tissue growth, muscle durability, bone strength, lung capacity, heart strength), I have become aware that, though the process is unseen and unfelt, when not adequately fed, the various parts of my body lose their strength, endurance, and efficiency. It is like operating a car with dirty oil, cheap gasoline, and insufficient lubrication: the car will run. But eventually the engine will tire and lose its effectiveness before its time.

Our bodies are the same.

God created our bodies to be keenly in tune with our emotions and our spiritual condition. Anger, frustration, sin, loneliness, and an unforgiving heart all affect our bodies as well. And the consequences of such emotions run deep. Rarely can you point to a direct cause-and-effect relationship, saying, "My ulcer today is a result of my anger and anxiety last month."

So it works with what we eat. The relationship between our food intake and our overall condition is not something one can necessarily see clearly overnight. There are many, many factors involved—exercise, emotions, metabolism, weight, heredity—in addition to food. Diligent care and thoughtfulness for the Christian must extend through many aspects of life.

Once my wife and I began to see the importance of health as God intended it, we realized that for years we had been part of a society hopelessly geared toward wrong nutrition. Supermarkets (and indeed, the entire food processing industry) are geared toward taste, convenience, appearance, and cost. Nutritional contents is a low priority. Gigantic corporations process food for quick sale and high profits.

Everything from baby food to ice cream contain a high concentration of chemicals, some of them harmful. White flour and sugar (refined to the point where the nutrition is not just low—it is gone!) had been the staples of our diet. As we looked around us it was hard to find *anything* not containing either white flour, refined sugar, chemicals or preservatives. We found no comfort in "unbleached" or "wheat" flour products or in "brown" or "kleenraw" sugars either. For some authorities firmly warn us that these are every bit as refined as the "white" varieties. The few things we were able to find that were somewhat "healthy" weren't overly pleasing to the palate. Along with everything else, our taste buds have been wrongly conditioned as well!

The more we read and the more we analyzed the diet we had grown accustomed to, the more we had to face the fact that most of the foods we had long been eating were nutritionally valueless. Our bodies were being run on the extras we acquired almost accidentally—the milk we poured over our cereal, the cream in our coffee, the carrot stick we had for lunch, the apple we had in the middle of the afternoon, the peas we ate alongside the dish of spaghetti for dinner. The "main courses" of the day did nothing for our bodies— the bowl of cereal, the velveeta sandwich followed by a handful of cookies and potato chips, the evening's spaghetti. We found that 75% of our food budget was essentially being thrown away and our bodies were existing on less than 25% of what actually went into them.

Over the years our bodies had grown accustomed to this. When I was living on dry cereal, white-bread sandwiches of peanut butter (one thing that is good for me) and brown sugar, donuts and coffee, I felt okay most of the time. Later when I tried to eat wheat germ for breakfast, my wrongly programmed system rebelled from my stomach to my colon.

But that our bodies had become accustomed to improper foods was no justification for continuing to eat them. My wife and I continued to look at the evidence before us and had to admit that our thinking and our eating habits needed to be reoriented. We saw it as a step of obedient responsibility—as part of our stewardship to God, our witness to others, and our preparation for the future.

Everywhere we read there are universal pronouncements against "the big three"—white flour, refined sugar, and chemical additives.

Concerning white flour:

A century ago the high-speed roller mill came into existence. The process made milling highly profitable; it enabled millers to ship flour, baked goods, cereals, and other products to any part of the world because they did not spoil. They did not spoil because the processing successfully removed the germ containing almost all the minerals and vitamins, approximately twenty known beneficial elements, which make flour the staff of life . . . it is altogether possible that early manufacturers did not realize to what extent they were robbing consumers of essential nutritional elements. The story today, however, is entirely different. Tremendous research has been done . . . [which has] turned up massive evidence of the nutritional deficiencies of refined flour.

Today, refined flour not only has the germ removed, but an assortment of twenty different chemicals and bleaching agents are used to further alter the original food value of flour, breads, cereals, pastas, cakes, and mixes we eat today. Pitifully few vitamins and minerals are replaced, but industry has conjured up such adjectives as "enriched" and "fortified" to give the impression that all are replaced. . . . The refining of carbohydrates, particularly flour and sugar, inflict[s] concentrated products on the body which the body was never designed to handle.[5]

And refined sugar:

There is no need to follow a piece of sugar cane through all the various complications of the refining process, but here are some of the substances used to produce those sparkling white crystals: lime, phosphoric acid, special clays known as diatomaceous earth, bone char, boneblack or animal charcoal. . . . In producing lactose or milk sugar which is used mainly in infant foods, "the whey is first clarified with lime, decolorized with carbon and then concentrated and crystalized." . . . In refining beet sugar, lime, carbon dioxide and sulfur dioxide are involved in the "purification" process. . . .

Refined sugar . . . is now regarded nutritionally as a diluting agent of the modern diet. . . . Thus, the more sugar consumed, the less opportunity for getting essential nutrients into the diet . . . low blood sugar makes individuals susceptible to polio. Low blood sugar is brought about by eating sugar, paradoxical as this may sound. . . . Recommending a diet . . . [forbidding all forms of refined sugar] Dr. Abrahamson relates spectacular cures for asthma, alcoholism, neuroses, fatigue, rheumatic fever, ulcers, epilepsy, depression. . . . [6]

And additives:

There is no question that the increased use of chemicals has brought a bonanza to the food industry . . . synthetic chemicals are much cheaper substitutes for flavors and colors than real fruits and vegetables and . . . the profit on synthetic foods formulated from chemicals is enormous.

Additives do several things: they lengthen shelf life, they make processed foods, and low-grade ingredients more palatable and eye-pleasing, they prevent spoilage, and according to Dr. Verrett, they mask deterioration. . . . Additives allow the manufacturer to put less of the natural ingredient into his product. . . . "Making food appear what it is not is an integral part of the $125 billion food industry. The deception ranges from surface packaging to the integrity of the food products' quality to the very shaping of food tastes." (Nader—p. 44)

In 1974, Dr. E. Cheraskin told us that we were eating ten pounds of additives [a year per person in the United States.] . . . we have no idea of the cumulative effect on living tissue, especially after years of consumption.

Beatrice Trum Hunter informs us that "some additives produce chemical changes in the food itself by altering the biological structure. Chemical food additives which produce derangements in the human system are so insidious that they do not become apparent until long after the original exposure . . . many chemicals, including food additives and pesticides, produce the same biological effects as atomic radiation, and are known as radiomimetic chemicals, because they mimic similar effects." (Hunter—pp. 45-46)

There are 2,764 classifications of intentional food additives, 1876 of which are from coal-tar derivatives. . . . The same dyes are used for clothing as for food. . . . We do not realize how many compounds are involved in imitating flavors . . . artificial pineapple takes seventeen compounds and imitation coffee flavor takes from two to three hundred! [7]

Reading such things certainly got our attention. And it wasn't as if we had to search for confirmation that these charges were true. Everywhere we turned was overwhelming evidence from many, many studies which said, essentially, that white flour, refined sugar, and food additives not only lack any nutritive benefit; they may be slowly and subtly poisoning our bodies. We read that food dyes caused cancer in animals; BHA and BHT (banned in many countries but allowed in the U.S. "to preserve freshness" and found in so many foods we could easily eat them at every meal) produced severe metabolic stress; nitrates and nitrites, used for years to cure meats, are among the most toxic chemicals found in our food supply and are regarded by many experts as purely poisonous.

"What else can we conclude?" we thought. The evidence was too overwhelming to ignore. We had to change our eating habits—even if it had nothing to do with preparing for Jesus' coming and was for no other reason than pure physical health. And so we began to make a concerted effort to work into our diet more healthful, natural, less refined foods.

"Natural" Foods

Many fadists are today calling for a "return to nature." Obviously such a thing as an end in itself has little value. But as a Christian I see two important reasons to heed their advice. First of all, God designed our food and our entire existence in the natural state. That God was concerned with what we eat is evidenced in His second statement to Adam after He had created him: "I have given you the seed-bearing plants throughout the earth, and all the fruit trees for your food" (Gen. 1:29, TLB). Since that time our ancestors have lived off the land in one way or another down through the centuries.

Naturally, buying and selling of food have gone on for many years. But the modern supermarket where food is boxed, packaged, and preserved for long periods is a distinctly modern invention. Imagine a seventeenth-century farmer, accustomed to the outdoor market where food was recognizable, entering a market today? I doubt if he would even know where he was. God created fruits, vegetables, grains, nuts, and herbs to be eaten as close to the natural state as possible.

Secondly, we no doubt of necessity will in the coming days be forced to return to nature simply to survive, even if that means nothing more than growing carrots, potatoes and peas in our backyard.

Healthful, natural, nutritious eating is becoming, for whatever reason, a priority in our lives. In the case of Judy and me, we see it as our attempt at obedience to the natural laws God established when He made the world and set man in it. We know full well that we cannot do away with the undesirable aspects of modern "progress." My wife shops at the supermarket and often has no choice but to buy items containing questionable ingredients. A strict legalism about this would be self-defeating and would serve to make a god out of a "health food fad." But to the extent we are able to adhere to natural foods and sound eating practices, we know we are separating ourselves by that small amount from the world systems (in this specific case, the processed food industry) and therefore are lessening our dependence on it. The fringe benefit from all this, of course, is that we are healthier, feel better, and will be physically more productive.

An added note here, however, is this: I've been the victim of too many pat answers to tell you *you'll feel great the moment you start eating better*! You may. But then again you may not. Our motive must be to follow the wise and prudent course regarding the food we eat. You should feel better eventually, but don't count on overnight changes. Just think of how long you've been eating unwholesome foods! I still find myself plagued with doubts when a common cold devastates me for a week. "I'm a Christian and I'm eating well. Why, Lord, do I feel so lousy?!" (My doctor assures me the reason is that my three preschool boys act like magnets for every germ in town.) Anyway, take it from me, you'll only be disappointed if you expect the changes in your eating habits to work rapid and miraculous transformations. This is a matter primarily of obedience to natural and scriptural principles.

So what then is natural eating?

Simply stated, it is eating food as closely as possible to the original ("natural") state. I've seen the phrase "living foods" used to describe the most healthy sort. Of course it is impossible to eat something that is still actually living, because the mere picking, cooking, uprooting, or preparing removes it from its natural living state. Yet the concept is valuable and we should remember that the closer our foods are in time to when they were still alive and growing, the more dynamic will be the nutrients they contain. An apple off the tree or a carrot from the ground is obviously in a more potent state than ones that have been lying on a grocer's shelf for some days. Remember, that carrot probably spent some time in a truck or railcar before that.

In this natural, living sense, then, fruits, vegetables, nuts, and seeds can be considered the top of the line. God created them to be eaten just as they are. Cooking removes foods one step from their strict natural state. Obviously, it cannot be completely avoided, but cook vegetables gently when you must and save the water for a soup or stew. (Probably half the nutrients cook into the pan.)

Wise eating does not preclude foods that must be altered, cooked, or mixed. Grains, for instance, must be ground, mixed, and baked to become bread; rice must be cooked; soybeans must be processed to be eaten in the many forms they are available. But in such cases, you must be careful that the processing is done "naturally"—not in some huge plant where the form of the grains is usually altered.

Our bodies need protein, but it is doubtful we require it in the quantities we've been told. Millions in the world live on a fraction of the protein Americans consume. A "high protein diet" is unnecessary (and possibly even harmful), but a balanced amount of regular protein is necessary for good cell growth. If you eat plenty of natural foods and dairy products, you will obtain the necessary protein—

whole grain breads, grains, milk, cheese, beans, and nuts. There is much controversy in health food circles over the subject of meat in the diet. In the original garden God did not provide animals for man to kill and eat. That came later, after the Fall. But it is clear that meat eating was accepted ever after and that the Lord ate meat as well. Peter's vision in Acts 10 seems to eliminate any spiritual significance in abstaining from meat.

It is interesting to note that when God instructed His people in Exodus and Leviticus concerning the eating of meat, He divided it into two categories and strictly forbade them to eat what He called "unclean" meats—those from animals with cloven hoofs but which do not chew their cuds, or vice versa. (A list of allowable and forbidden animals, fish, and birds is given by God in Leviticus 11 and in Deuteronomy 14.) In recent times medical doctors and knowledgeable scientists have found these (as well as all of God's instructions to the Jews) to be medically, emotionally, and morally sound (see *None of These Diseases* by McMillan, Fleming H. Revell Co.). God's commands were always for His people's absolute best. We can conclude therefore that His identification of certain meats as unclean had a definite physical basis.

Nutritionalists do warn that meat which takes the place of more natural foods will overload our diet with too much protein. They are in fairly universal agreement that fish is the most beneficial of all.

Soybeans are a terrific protein. My wife has learned, through much practice (serving soybeans tastefully is an art that must be acquired), to make an outstanding soybean soup which is heavy on rice, barley, and many vegetables. We have it nearly once a week. She also makes a soybean pie (from soybean pulp, eggs, milk, honey, and whole wheat flour) that is nearly identical to pumpkin. We are just now discovering the variety of ways to use tofu, another soybean product.

Dairy products (milk, eggs, cheese, yogurt, etc.) is another area where nutritionalists disagree. I've read many things on both sides and my conclusion is that any theory which becomes so elevated in importance to cause one to lose balanced perspective is overstressed. Moderation in these grey areas will usually keep you from going too far wrong, along with scriptures such as found in the latter half of 1 Corinthians 10.

While white, puffy, "enriched" bread is one of the worst things we can give our systems, whole grain bread (and things made from whole grain flours) are among the best. The bran, germ, and fiber are the "miracle" ingredients in every grain of wheat, barley, or rye. Processed and refined flours and breads (even those that say fortified or enriched) have removed either all or part of these essentials. When baking, use only whole grain flour (one that is obtained simply from grinding the grains themselves into flour—no processing, nothing added, nothing removed). You can buy flour made this way or you can buy the kernels of grain themselves, a flour mill, and grind your own.

Bread made with whole grain flour is truly a *food*, not merely a slab with which to cover something else. There are infinite bread recipes, as individual and fun to experiment with as there are people to try them. And eating wisely does not necessarily mean forever abstaining from cakes and cookies and the like. We still enjoy such things, and eat them knowing we are obtaining beneficial nutrients for our bodies at the same time—because we thoughtfully analyze everything that goes into such recipes, using whole grain flour.

Vitamins and minerals are important as well. In our present society it is nearly impossible, no matter how natural our diet, to obtain all our bodies need. Even our "natural" foods have often lost a great deal because we have had to buy them in places far removed from the actual growing process. And time does destroy many nutrients. Fruits and vegetables are not usually fresh, nuts we eat from a can, grains and flours have been trucked over long distances. Adding supplements to your diet can help fill in the gaps some of these deficiencies create. It is important not to make vitamins and minerals your supreme goal for good health. They are simply one additional factor in a total health program. You will usually obtain much of what you need if you are eating the proper foods. If you do decide to take vitamins, get good strong ones from a health food store, not the sugar-coated, drugstore variety. A good multiple vitamin in addition to vitamins C, E, and B complex along with your daily dosage of brewer's yeast (The health food people will tell you, "You'll learn to love it!" But don't believe it. Just mix it with your juice and drink up. Your body loves it despite the taste.) will usually suffice unless you have some specific deficiency. The walls of a health food store are lined with hundreds of varieties. As I said before, don't think vitamins will solve all your ills. They won't. But along with everything else, they should help.

A recommendation before we continue: consult further sources for additional information and study on these subjects. Beware of the author who says, "*This* will be the answer . . ." or another, "*This* remedy is the cure-all. . . ." Be nutritionally aware and well-read and informed. And always remember Paul's advice: "Food will not commend us to God" (1 Cor. 8:8, RSV)," . . . whatever you do, do all to the glory of God" (1 Cor. 10:31, RSV). Not to discount all we have said regarding our physical stewardship, but simply to remind us that unless our hearts and spirits are in their right place before our Father, everything else we do will be pointless.

Specific Guidelines Toward Wise Eating

If by this time you think you might like to make some alterations in your eating habits, what follows are the general guidelines we have come to use in our home.

As we've already discussed, I would encourage you to eat as much in the natural state as possible. This would include lots of fruits and vegetables (fresh whenever you can get them) and their juices, nuts, dried fruits, seeds, sprouts, and grains. Wheat can be boiled and eaten like rice; barley is great in soups. Natural cereals (homemade granola—there are many different varieties—experiment!) made with wheat germ, rolled oats, nuts, seeds, coconut, honey, are great. Raw vegetables and salads should be eaten regularly.

I feel that your goal should be to completely rid your house of sugar and refined flour. If the storm of protest from your family overwhelms you, make a gradual changeover by using part whole wheat flour in your recipes. Honey can be substituted for sugar in most anything by simply adding 1/2 to 3/4 in honey what the recipe calls for in sugar (honey varies in strength) and then cut the liquid content of the remainder of the recipe by about 1/4 of a cup. Sometimes you'll also need to add 1/4 teaspoon of baking powder or baking soda for the consistency of your batter.

Baking done with whole grain flour may take some getting used to. When we began several years ago, my wife quickly tired of my unimaginative comment after sampling many of her "healthy" desserts, "This tastes like dog food." Our cookies were more like muffins; pancakes were so thick and grainy I could barely manage to eat one per meal.

But two things gradually changed. Our "junk food" conditioning turned around. And Judy, through diligent practice, learned techniques that enabled her to make really magnificent healthy things. Her homemade granola is infinitely superior to anything I've ever had from a store. I can't resist her cookies when she makes a batch. Even confirmed white-flour addicts marvel at the taste. She has experimented and come up with some really ingenious things— cheese breads, sprout bread, carob-pero bars, tofu casseroles, and so on. And we guiltlessly eat these healthy things (sweets included) knowing we are getting nothing but flour, eggs, honey, milk, and a few extras—all natural ingredients. It is best not to overdo such "bready" things— too many carbohydrates, no matter how natural, can have an adverse effect. But being able to enjoy desserts really serves to round out the menu. I must confess, my sweet tooth hasn't disappeared.

The byword here is practice. When you first try to convert your household over, it is going to be tough even if you are all in it together. Get some good books on the subject, some cookbooks that have sugarless recipes, and then experiment. Soon you will wonder where all this good food has been all your life.

In the midst of the fun of experimenting and talk of good food, we must remember why such measures are vital. We want our bodies to be in top shape for the Lord's return. It isn't that we know honey will be available then and sugar won't—it could be the other way around. Our motivation comes from wanting to be diligent managers of the magnificent body God so lovingly gave us. We want to provide it with the most complete and useful fuel possible.

Once you've eaten the right foods, your body must be able to utilize them efficiently and convert the nutrients into energy and strength. Therefore digestion is an additional key to health. There are several things you can do to aid your digestive system.

Drink plenty of liquids, but not with meals if you can help it. Avoid drinking 1/2 hour before and after each meal. Chew thoroughly, eat slowly, and don't eat when you are emotionally worked up. All these things will help your digestive juices work more effectively. If your digestive organs must overwork at every meal, they will tire quickly. And if your food is not thoroughly digested, your entire system will suffer—stomach, colon, liver, kidneys, to the bowels.

Digestion is also aided when you eat as few different types of food at the same time as possible. Each food group requires different chemicals in the digestive process. Proteins, heavy starches and carbohydrates is probably one of the worst combinations. We must be reasonable about this—you cannot restructure your entire day around your meals. But the more you can follow this principle the less you will suffer from gas and acid and ineffective digestion. For instance, eat a breakfast or lunch consisting mostly of fruits and a dinner comprised of vegetables and proteins. Combine varieties within the larger food groups whenever possible.

The many varieties of cultured milk—yogurt, keifer, buttermilk, felia, and acidophilus—are also great aids to digestion and should be eaten or drunk regularly. They have great nutritional content as well. Be creative in the ways you discover to enjoy these things. And like bread, you can make your own. A spoonful or two of the old batch in a quart of milk and overnight you'll have a new batch. Yogurt is a little more difficult, involving heating the milk and a few additional ingredients. There are a variety of recipes and methods. Again—experiment! Learning these skills takes time, effort, and practice.

Another bit of advice concerning digestion and eating habits in general (which advice I am struggling to apply)—eat less! Most of us eat far more than we need and as a result have accumulated a host of additional problems. Stuffing ourselves is a sure way to overwork many of our internal organs. No matter how healthy the food we eat may be, if our bodies get too much of it all at once, our systems won't be able to digest it. Not only will the food not get properly used, but our bodies will be unnecessarily taxed. Keeping our bodies trim is a part of our stewardship as well and is an indication of a healthy body that is utilizing its food well. Being overweight is a symptom of more than just overeating; it is a sign that the food we eat is not being efficiently used in our bodies.

Stimulants such as coffee (tea—debatable), drugs, and alcohol should be used sparingly if at all. Smoking is out for anyone seriously concerned with his health. Pain killers and many things we Americans keep in our medicine cabinets (aspirin, Tums, Malox, Rolaids, Contac, sleeping pills, tranquilizers, Anacin, Nyquil, cough syrup, Bufferin, and on and on and on) are unnatural and should be avoided. There are times, of course, when medicine is needed. I am thankful for the medications we have had to fight virus and infection in our boys. But we must get away from using drugs and pills whenever we have a stomachache or a headache. These things upset the chemical balances within our bodies, balances which if left alone will allow the body to eventually repair itself. God built amazing healing properties into our bodies to handle what goes wrong with them from time to time. When we continually try to circumvent those natural processes with artificial substances, we interfere with God's method of dealing with it. We also render our bodies less capable of responding to natural healing in the future.

Lastly, and possibly as important as anything, is this: take time to notice labels on cans and boxes in the market. Look for sugar content, chemicals, and preservatives. They are in almost everything. You'll be amazed when you begin to scrutinize the fine print. But by shopping carefully you can learn to avoid such products.

Some Wider Implications of Our Eating Habits

These attempts at wise eating are directly involved in our walk with the Lord and our diligent attempt to become a people "set apart," totally dependent on Him. Healthy eating for the Christian, though wise in itself, is part of glorifying God in every little detail of our lives.

As Judy and I have learned to view it in this way, all sorts of additional factors have become part of our culinary faithfulness. Food waste is an important issue. Creative use of leftovers, even small amounts, is a rewarding way to stop waste. And we are careful about not overeating just to "finish it up." We are more aware of our buying habits; economy, thoughtfulness, and thriftiness help us not only when shopping but also in the preparation of food. Though being careful with leftovers won't directly help those starving in Asia, such diligence can serve as a reminder that we are part of a large body of people, most of whom don't have our western abundance. I find myself remembering to pray more often for the people God has created everywhere and more conscious of my personal responsibility to feed and care for the poor in my own area. And also I give more thought to my financial responsibility to my family, spending money on food wisely and stretching food dollars wherever possible. What better preparation for the future than to become adept at economical food buying, preparation, and re-use? The practice and techniques we acquire now will pay dividends later.

For the woman, who is usually responsible for a family's

food preparation, the kitchen offers an ideal setting to learn to express God's imagination and creativity with her hands. When a woman creates original and economic dishes she accomplishes two things: she is arming herself for the days ahead and is providing enjoyment and good health for her family in the meantime. Making bread, yogurt, rolls, desserts, growing vegetables, and hand-picking apples to make applesauce not only helps to cut down on a monthly food bill but can also train a woman to depend less and less on the supermarket. A man whose wife diligently does these things (as listed in Proverbs 31) has, in the words of Solomon, "found a rare jewel." He does well to follow the injunction in the last verse of Proverbs and praise and bless her often for the many fine things she does.

Don't be taken in by all this "economy" talk, however; saving money will not be automatic. It requires hard work and planning in order to lower your food bill, especially if you intend to eat more healthfully. Generally speaking, it is more expensive to buy natural foods. You will find the packaged and processed things (though horrendously overpriced when you consider their nutritive content) easier, less time consuming, and often cheaper to prepare than the "natural" ones. Fruits, nuts, dried fruit, juices, cheese, and honey are all expensive items. The food industry is set up to mass produce the foods we are trying to avoid. So production costs are lower. Natural peanut butter costs more than the varieties with sugar; soybean margarine is priced higher than regular margarine; whole wheat bread is more expensive than white bread. To keep your bill in balance and especially to lower it will require wisdom and care.

There are economic advantages, however, which you can train yourself to incorporate into your planning. Several years ago the estimation was that $5 would buy approximately four pounds of beef in comparison to twenty-five pounds of soybeans. Not only that, the four pounds of beef contain a total of approximately 350 grams of protein while the soybeans have over 4,500 grams. The beef provides six servings, the soybeans 150. Furthermore, soybeans contain practically every known vitamin. So not only are they drastically cheaper than other forms of protein, they actually contain vastly more nutritional content as well.[8] From the standpoint of what you are actually getting with your money each month in terms of usefulness, some of the healthy eating *is* economical. Another aspect is that the money and time invested in well-chosen foods will in the long run be money saved through the years on doctor and dentist bills. (Though I was raised on few sweets and brushed my teeth regularly, I have suffered with cavities for as long as I can remember. I cannot remember a single no-cavity check-up up through the time when we were married. But almost from the moment we banned white flour and sugar from our home, they disappeared. I have not had a single cavity in over four years.)

A Day's Menu

Let's now take the things we've discussed so far and transfer them into a single day. We'll see how some of these principles can be incorporated into a daily schedule.

First let's consider breakfast. The classic American fare consists of some combination of the following: coffee, tea, dry cereal, hot cereal, toast, eggs, bacon, sausage, waffles, pancakes, French toast, milk, biscuits, ham, grits, juice, jam, hash browns, or fruit. More than likely you had some of these things this morning and usually do. Let's look at it.

Several things should probably go—the coffee and dry cereal are the first. The bacon and sausage most likely are processed beyond recognition; chemicals, preservatives and unheard of things (some you would rather not know about) are sometimes added. The ham is debatable—remember to read the label for additives and chemicals used in the curing process. Jam from a store will have more sugar content than fruit. Making your own with honey is a great alternative.

A few changes here and there and you'll have a delightfully healthy breakfast. Fresh fruits and fruit juices are wonderful and canned are fine unless there are suspicious words on the label such as "artificially flavored," "imitation," "sweetened," "fruit-flavored drink," etc. *Always* carefully read the label; buy nothing but pure juice. The toast, biscuits, hotcakes, waffles, and so on, are good if you make them with whole wheat flour and honey. Mixes, white flour, sugar, and syrup are nutritionally unsafe. Your system will have a much easier time digesting a bowl of fruit than it will a heavy mixture of hotcakes. So even though they may have some healthy ingredients, don't make a steady diet of such things. Good substitutes for jams and syrups are honey, molasses, peanut butter, fruit, and apple-sauce.

Eggs are fine, so are hash browns (try them with the skin on when you grate the potatoes). Hot cereal is good as well if it's a whole grain cereal without additives. Homemade granola is a great addition to breakfast and wheat germ with half-and-half can be a treat too. Variety can be added by occasionally serving a large bowl of fruit with dried figs, prunes, apricots, peaches, and dates. A dish of yogurt with strawberries, sliced peaches, raspberries, or melons is a nice change too.

Really, it won't be so hard. There's endless opportunity for variety. A good breakfast is not necessarily huge. You could have fruit one morning, granola the next, hotcakes or waffles the next, yogurt and fruit, eggs and whole wheat toast, hot cereal, and so on. (I always drink some brewer's yeast in a glass of orange juice prior to breakfast.) Experiment with different combinations and enjoy your first meal of the day.

(I wrote these last several pages early in the morning. I got up from that last sentence, and walked downstairs to find my wife mixing a batch of hotcakes; ingredients—eggs, soy oil, corn meal, yellow cheese, bran, and cottage cheese. And with peaches on top . . . Aahh!)

On to lunch. Most Americans are used to a sandwich of some kind (or a hamburger, hot dog, taco) with all sorts of things on the side—French fries, malts, cookies, potato chips. School lunches are notoriously weak nutritionally—mostly processed, pre-prepared, and starchy (lunch meats, white bread, casseroles full of preservatives, sugar-filled snacks and beverages, hot dogs, and so on). Ice cream is very common fare for most youngsters. Teenagers live on soft drinks and hamburger stand "junk." Working men and women run to the delicatessen for a spicy sandwich, bag of chips, and Coke. Lunch is probably the most devastating meal of the day for our poor bodies.

Next time you are thinking of ordering a hot dog, consider this:

> Nitrate and Nitrite (saltpeter) has been used for many years in curing meat and is found in ham, bacon, luncheon meats, canned meat and fish, as well as in frankfurters. . . . There has been a war waging against their use because it has been found that nitrite (contained in nitrate) is one of the most toxic chemicals in our food supply. . . . In regard to hot dogs, bacon, bologna, and smoked fish, Dr. Lijinsky says, "In my opinion nitrites constitute our worst cancer problem. I don't touch any of that stuff when I know nitrite has been added."[9]

When you think of getting a soft drink to go with your lunch or are buying breakfast ("Vitamin C enriched") drinks for your family, remember this:

> A smattering of random newspaper headlines provides an ominous warning: "Americans Eat Fungicide-Treated Lemons Banned in Japan," "Hundreds of Thousands of Cancer-Causing Chemicals Out of Control Threaten Consumers," "Lead Poisoning Reexamined," "Technologists Seek Longest Shelf Life," "Sodium Nitrite Produces Brain Changes," "Government Approving Thousands of Food Additives That Threaten Your Health. . . ," etc.
>
> One autumn day the news media announced that Red Dye No. 2 [only ONE of a host of harmful food additives we eat daily] was found to be carcinogenic [cancer-causing]. The dye was ordered off the market, but the food processing plants complained that they had no workable substitute. The dye remained on the market for many months in soft drinks, fruit drinks, cereals, desserts, diet desserts, candy, and miscellaneous items.

The dye, produced from beetles' egges imported from Central America, was used in Fanta grape, strawberry, red creme soda, and cherry soft drinks. It was also used in Tang, Kool-Aid, Hi-C grape, Wyler's low-calorie fruit drink mixes, Royal gelatins, Life-Savers in raspberry, grape, and cherry flavors, Open-Pit barbecue sauce, and certain soups. Lipstick, strawberry ice cream, and many other commodities were contaminated by Red Dye No. 2. Unfortunately, workable substitutes have not been found for all items, so the dye is still a part of the food we eat.[10]

And this says nothing about the *other* ingredients in these foods. Imagine the sugar content of soft drinks! A Coke is mostly pure sugar, terrible for your system and even worse for your teeth!

And when you are ordering an ice cream cone or trying to decide which flavor of ice cream to buy to serve your family tonight after dinner with cookies, think of this:

The food in your market basket contains artificial flavor enhancers, preservatives, antioxidants, emulsifiers, stabilizers, thickeners, acidulants, colors, bleaching, maturing agents, humectants (to keep food moist), anticaking agents, clarifying agents, curing agents, foaming agents, foam inhibitors, and non-nutritive sweeteners.

For example, Americans consume 800 million gallons of ice cream each year. Most give little thought to the ingredients, not knowing they are digesting a small chemical laboratory. Ice cream manufacturers are not required to label these additives which include: *Piperonal*, used instead of vanilla. This is a chemical used to kill lice. *Aldehyde C17*, a flavor for cherry ice cream. It is an inflammable liquid used also in anilene dyes, plastic, and rubber. *Diethyl Glucol*, an inexpensive chemical used as an emulsifier in place of eggs. Diethyl Glucol is the same substance used in anti-freeze and in paint removers. *Ethyl Acetate* gives ice cream a pineapple flavor. It's a chemical used also to clean leather and textiles. Its vapors have caused chronic lung, liver, and heart damage. *Butyraldehyde* gives ice cream a nut flavor. It is also used in rubber cement. *Amyl Acetate* provides a banana flavor, and is a chemical also used as an oil paint solvent. *Benzyl Acetate* in ice cream gives it a strawberry flavor. It is a nitrite solvent.

Come and get it, folks! The fresh, tangy flavor of butylated hydroxytoluene . . . the home-cooked goodness of calcium disodium *Edta* . . . the satisfying richness of sodium carboxymethylcellulose. . . .[11]

It is humorous to be sure, yet we have here a deadly serious issue. In the face of such evidence it has not been difficult for our family to firmly equate our spiritual faithfulness and bodily stewardship with our eating habits. Even if it were possible to somehow rationalize the mistreating our own adult bodies, my wife and I have found it impossible to rationalize away the effect on the bodies of our children. Consider the baby foods that are given to so many young children:

Early in 1975 a government-sponsored committee of nutritionists, physicians, and citizen activists conducted a study on infant feeding practices. . . . [They] charged that manufacturers were adding such substances as sugar, salt, monosodium glutamate, spices, sodium nitrite (an element linked to cancer in animals) and large amounts of water to enhance flavor and appearance and thereby increase sales. . . .
In August, 1975, the Consumers Union produced an alarming report. In thirty-nine commercial baby foods they found insect parts, rodent hairs, and paint chips. These three contaminants were found in 25 percent of the foods tested, compared with about 10 percent of the samples tested in 1972. The filth was found in foods made by Gerber, Heinz, and Beech-Nut. Beech-Nut beef with vegetables and cereal was the worst offender. About twenty chips per jar were found.[12]

Our diet does not have to contain such harmful elements. A mother can quite easily grind or blend food that she has prepared for her family and freeze in meal servings for her baby. There are natural substitutes for nearly everything; carob for chocolate; honey, barley-malt, molasses, or fruit sweeteners for sugars. And you can make your own ice cream, cookies, beverages, and candy, as well as baby food as we have suggested.

When it comes to preparing your own lunch (it will be hard to avoid the problems when buying lunch), here are a few reasonable changes. Sandwich breads must be whole-grain, and what goes between them is crucial—no Velveeta, bologna, or lunch meat. Try cheese, fish, egg, turkey, chicken. If you get these things from a can, remember; *read the label first!* An entire lunch of fruit is nice. I often take just a small bag of dried apricots, prunes, figs, and an apple to work with me. Yogurt is also a good addition to lunch. Or a lunch can be predominately vegetables: carrot sticks, celery, a big salad, sprouts. Roughage is extremely important in your diet and raw vegetables like this provide it. Nuts add variety. Toasted cheese sandwiches, soup in a thermos—the possibilities are almost endless.

If you buy your lunch out, particularly at some fast-food outlet, it is very difficult to avoid fried foods—French fries, chicken, onion rings, apple rings, fish, etc.

But remember that no matter how "healthy" the basic food may once have been—potatoes, chicken, apples, fish, etc.—the frying process does them irreparable harm. The heat of the frying process changes the composition of the oil, making it almost impossible for these fats to be assimilated into the bloodstream. Instead, they collect on your arterial walls and remain there. These hardened plaques are considered one of the major causes of heart attacks and strokes.

You are, therefore, much better off fixing your own lunch rather than buying it. And remember the ground rules—natural, simple, with a minimum of cooking and mixing of kinds.

As we move on to dinner we need to make many of the same necessary changes we found regarding lunch. The extensive meat eating, all that pasta in casseroles, the desserts and prepared or canned or ready-to-eat dishes should all be severely modified. Analyze the contents of anything you buy. How much process did it go through to get here on the shelf? How far away is it from where it was grown? What has been added to it in chemicals, coloring, preservatives? What has been taken away from it? The word "artificial" is a big, red warning signal.

We have found that our dinners fit better with our guidelines and priorities for health when we center them around the vegetables rather than some more filling main dish. Two vegetables are standard for us and we eat meat but rarely (we do have fish about once a week as well as some form of soybeans). Eating vegetables doesn't necessarily simply mean a little pile of peas on your plate. My wife has discovered recipes for spinach souffle, zucchini and cheese casserole, vegetable soups and stews, sauteed chicken and zucchini. We regularly have tomatoes fried in a batter of egg, flour, and wheat germ, and dishes which combine rice, cheese, and vegetables. Salads are an enjoyable obligation, containing lots of raw vegetables. How about an occasional supper of fruits and cottage cheese?

Dinner should be an enjoyable family meal, especially for the tired husband home from a hectic day. So, wives, it will take a good deal of godly and prayerful creativity to make a dinner of fish, broccoli, squash, and a salad exciting to your husband! But with practice, you can discover ways to accomplish just that. We mustn't get in a rut, either, of eating only those particular things we like best. To obtain balanced nutrition we should eat many types of foods. I can offer you no ready answers; the work that this requires is part of the price we must all pay for years of neglect and wrong eating habits. But believe me, there *are* ways to remain consistent with these healthful principles and also make meals exciting. I encourage you to find your own methods and recipes.

You will undoubtedly be tempted to give up many

times, but keep at it. Don't forget that we are preparing ourselves to be an attractive, well-nourished, faithful, conditioned Bride for Jesus when He comes. And in the process we're going to become healthier.

Husbands, don't make this only your wife's responsibility. It will never work unless both of you are in agreement on it. Commitment to natural eating is the foundation. Your leadership and support will sustain your wife as you both learn to change your eating patterns. She enjoys providing tasty dishes for you and your children. Help her in that natural God-given role by praising and encouraging her every effort. You'll reap the rewards of it many times over in better health and in delicious eating.

2

Fasting

A Lost Secret of Health

Taking care of your body is not merely giving it the proper nutrients as we have just discussed. There are three phases in the course toward optimum physical well-being. For any one of them to work fully, all three must be a regular part of your life. Providing your body the food it needs is but the initial step. For the protein, vitamins, minerals, and so on, to provide you with maximum nourishment and energy, two other processes must be regularly at work in your body as well. They will be the subjects of the following two chapters.

It may seem odd to follow a discussion of eating habits with one on fasting. Yet the two go hand-in-hand. It has been our discovery that without fasting healthy eating cannot accomplish its full results.

There has been a resurgence of interest in fasting among Christians in recent years and a number of books on the subject. Churches are beginning regular times of fasting and individuals are witnessing the spiritual power which fasting and prayer often can unlock. However, it has not been until very recently that a number of Christians have begun to discover the *physical* benefits of fasting, viewed as it has been until now almost exclusively as a spiritual exercise. But the physical side of fasting can be equally significant. As with many of God's instructions to the children of Israel, fasting is a discipline God required for a variety of reasons. Though it is largely foreign to our times and culture, fasting is found throughout the Bible, Old and New Testaments alike. At the time of Jesus the Jews were accustomed to fasting one day each week.

For centuries fasting has been regarded as a medically curing and rejuvenating measure. The father of medicine, Hippocrates, often prescribed it, as did many other of the great physicians of ancient times. Fasting has long been practiced by many of the world's great philosophers and thinkers in order to "attain mental and physical efficiency."

In recent years, however, particularly in the West, fasting has been out of vogue and nearly forgotten by the average person. It doesn't exactly fit the American way of life! Yet many doctors, especially in Europe, have begun scientific investigations into the therapeutic and healing results of fasting. There are a number of health spas, notably in Sweden, where fasting is being rediscovered as a most integral part of successful health therapy.

Fasting for a Christian contains a double blessing. When undertaken for spiritual reasons God is able greatly to use it. Though it is a mystery, fasting seems to add much power to prayer ("this kind can only come out by prayer and fasting"—Mark 9:29) and to one's devotional life ("the Spirit led him into the wilderness where he fasted for forty days . . . and the angels ministered to him"—Mark 1:12-13). Fasting is mentioned seventy-four times in the Bible and usually produced dramatic results when practiced as God instructed.

Many doctors and nutritionalists now prescribing fasting (in much the same way as did ancient physicians) as a significant aspect of physical healing, usually also suggest that it be accompanied by a greatly modified natural diet.

Fasting and improved eating habits, however, do not actually cure the body's ailments. They help the body cure itself. God built into the human body the most astounding healing processes known to man. When used in conjunction with one another, fasting and nutritious eating have a remarkable effect in supporting natural healing. Initially, the fast provides the body a much-needed rest from the digestive process. The body's organs can rejuvenate themselves and then devote their energies afterwards to the maintaining of maximum health, promoting self-healing when necessary.

But fasting does much more than simply rest the body. In the process, the elimination of old cells and toxins (secreted chemical poisons accumulating in the body) is sped up and the building of new, healthy cells is accelerated. It is an amazing process which God designed.

How a Fast Works

Because it is receiving no new nutrition, after three or four days on a fast your body will begin to burn its own tissues for the energy it needs. But these tissues are not burned indiscriminately. In His wisdom, God designed the process so that those cells and tissues which are aging, dead, damaged or diseased would be the first to go. In other words, when you fast your body feeds on the most inferior cells first; as it does these cells and the toxins found in them are eliminated from your body. Thus, contrary as it seems, your body as a whole is actually strengthened during a fast. This accounts for the amazing reports so often heard from people who have fasted for long periods. "I actually felt stronger the longer I went . . ."; "After the hunger disappeared around day seven, I had boundless energy . . . ," and so on.

Fat deposits are among the first to be eliminated and before long the process speeds up the building of new, healthy cells. During a fast the purifying and cleansing capacities of the eliminative systems, such as the liver, kidneys, lungs, and skin, are increased. The liver and the kidneys are among the most complex and versatile organs in the body—next to the brain in complexity. They are the organs that detoxify and neutralize all the chemicals that are unknowingly poured into the body and dispose of them as much as possible through elimination.

In recent years we have tremendously overburdened these organs with the more than three thousand chemicals and additives we ingest. During a fast these organs not only get a well-deserved rest but the drinking water (which is one of the most vital factors in a fast) passing through them flushes out collected toxins and waste materials which have accumulated in our bodies over the years. In the process of burning inferior cells or cells where wastes have gathered, much of this bodily debris is loosened and expelled and some is burned for energy as well. The eliminative organs are able to miraculously cleanse the body of these wastes because they are relieved of their usual burden of food digestion, concentrating on the removal of these old wastes and chemical poisons.

Because of this miraculous cleansing process which a fast initiates inside the body, it truly can be a healing measure. As we mentioned, there are hundreds of clinics and spas in Germany and Sweden where fasting is now employed on a grand scale as the primary means of healing. Dr. Otto H. F. Buchiner of Germany and his father, in fifty years of medical practice, have supervised over 80,000 fasts for nearly every known condition of ill health.[13] There are documented cases of healing through fasting for the following: weak heart, colitis, arthritis, premature aging, gallstones, high blood pressure, neuritis, emphysema, back pain, chronic headaches, asthma, psoriasis, bronchitis, tonsilitis, enlargement of the prostate gland, and nervous stress. (See *Are You Confused?*, listed in appendix.) In addition, fasting is the most effective method of weight reduction known. Overweight people have a shorter life expectancy and are more susceptible to diabetes, high blood pressure, heart failure, arteriosclerosis, gallbladder disease, varicose veins, hernias, headaches, fatigue, irritability, sleeping difficulty, shortness of breath, and indigestion. For many, fasting would quickly remove a number of these symptoms.

There have been some truly remarkable discoveries recently about the effects of diet (along with fasting) to cure various illnesses. Dr. Carey Reams has predicted heart attacks with accuracy and has seen other patients avoid attacks from a change in diet.[14] Eydie Mae in *How I Conquered Cancer Naturally* tells how she reversed a serious case of late-stage terminal cancer strictly through a drastically altered diet. There are hundreds of other examples which boast of healings due to changed diet. And in many cases, the supervising dietician, physician, or nutritionalist prescribes a fast to start the procedure. Everyone who has seen healings of this sort unanimously says, "The food and the fast do not heal. They simply give the body the most efficient fuel possible and the most effective means for allowing it to carry out its own miraculous healing functions." God created the human body more capable and complex than the most sophisticated computer man has yet devised. No hospital or doctor can give you the expertise God gave each one of our bodies inherently. (See *Jesus Wants You Well*, listed in appendix.)

A word of explanation here. Fasting and wise eating are the foundation for nearly every kind of healing. But there are no blanket rules that will work for every person with every sort of ailment. Everybody is different, every person's background is different, and every situation has different requirements. The guidelines I set forth regarding wise eating are only general principles; they are not intended as prescription for any specific ailments.

For instance, in Eydie Mae's cancer-combating diet, her list of forbidden foods included: all dairy products, honey, fish, vitamins, and dried fruit—all things I recommended.[15] This apparent inconsistency results from the fact that the healing of specific diseases is a highly specialized thing and should not be equated with general eating habits. You will usually see many similarities, but there will always be exceptions.

Adhere, therefore, to these principles of wise eating and

fasting for all-around health and well-being. But when you are undertaking a nutrition-based remedy for some particular thing, make certain you do ample research. Physicians who can knowledgeably prescribe a diet for healing are rare. But there are other sources: public nurses, clinics for diabetics, books, etc. For ailments less severe than cancer, experiment with various diets and methods. Expect results to come slowly. Read and study, not letting yourself get swept in by pat answers.

Methods of Fasting

So there are certainly convincing reasons in the physical realm why fasting should become a regular part of our routine. For Americans, doing so is even more crucial. We are a grossly overfed (yet often undernourished) people. A large portion of the population is overweight to some degree or another. Even when we are trying to apply principles of wise eating, our tendency from years past is to eat too much.

There are differing theories about the kinds of fasting which are the most physically beneficial. Christians have traditionally adhered to the "water only" fast as being the most total and therefore valuable spiritually. One is made keenly aware of bodily deprivation and hunger and one's need to trust in God.

However, most European fasting specialists today favor fruit and vegetable juice and broth fasts. They reason that such juices continue to give the body needed nutrition while at the same time allow the digestive system to turn itself to the cleansing work of the fast. Liquid adds no burden to the digestive system and therefore actually promotes the healing process. One of the most important aspects of a liquid fast is that you are enabled to fast for much longer periods of time at near full physical capacity, thus benefitting from longer periods of toxin and waste elimination from your body. There is a case on record of a woman who fasted at the Stobhill General Hospital in Glasgow for 249 days on liquids. She lost 1/4 of her previous weight and a painful arthritic condition was cleared up completely.[16]

Since there are advocates of various kinds of fasts, why not fast several ways? Advantages from different kinds can be put to work in your own body.

Breaking a fast is a very important aspect if it is to have its full and most beneficial effects. Fasts should be broken slowly, taking up to three or four days for a fast of two weeks or more. You should begin with easily digestible foods such as fruits and fruit juices (if you've been on a strict water fast, your entire first day should probably be juices). You should then ease into greater quantities of fruit and slowly add yogurt, salads, soups, and so on. Remember, since your digestive system has been on vacation, go easy on it. Keep in mind too the other factors for good digestion—drinking liquids between meals, little mixing of foods, etc.

Throughout the fast, wastes that have been dislodged within your body are making their way through your organs until they are eliminated. By breaking a fast too quickly you will instantly halt this process. The wastes and toxins, therefore, that are still working out of your body will be absorbed back into your system before they have had the chance to be completely eliminated. This is why laxative foods are the best to begin with: fruits, roughage, bran, juice—they continue the flushing process so as to allow most of these toxins to be removed before your body fully resumes its normal functions.

Fasting—Spiritual Preparation

Though the physical effects of fasting are marvelous, the spiritual power released can be even greater. In the Bible fasting had the power to change the course of the history of nations. Jesus fasted before facing His most severe encounters with the enemy. Derek Prince tells us as well of examples in recent times where fasting has altered events having national significance.[17] Arthur Wallis details many of the ways God can use a fast in our personal lives to bring us into deeper levels of communion with Him.[18] Fasting has awesome power of many kinds.

As Christians we have the exciting opportunity of fasting for both physical and spiritual reasons. The European health spas may boast remarkable healings—and I do not doubt them. But what could parallel the total physical *and* spiritual fast as we allow God to do a cleansing and rejuvinating work throughout our bodies while He also cleanses and purifies our spirits?

What does all this have to do with our preparation for the future?

As we've previously noted, when the time of hardships come we are going to need healthy bodies to endure. Fasting is simply one additional means toward the optimun health and vigor those times will necessitate. But even more importantly, when shortages and even famine does come to the world, we may often be forced to fast from sheer lack of food. It will be the person who through years of diligent and prayerful practice is well accustomed to fasting who will be able to stand strong through such times with a minimum of difficulty and personal hardship.

Some might think that the best preparation would be to eat a lot while it's available so as to store up "extra" calories and energy and fuel for the body. Then when hard times strike, there would be plenty of fuel "stored up" for the days of shortage. This is the world's way of looking at impending crises: get all you can now so you will have plenty put aside. The Children of Israel made the same fatal error by trying to hoard the manna in the wilderness.

But it doesn't work that way. God's ways usually run cross-current to man's ways, and the preparation fasting provides for future hard times is a clear example. Consider two men as examples. One is overweight, accustomed to eating whatever he wants, and out of shape. The other is thin. He lives on fruits and vegetables and other natural foods, exercises regularly and vigorously and is well used to fasting. If you put both men on a twenty-day fast, what would happen?

The large man would soon wear down emotionally and physically, probably within a day or two. His body would not be used to such treatment. The experience would be new to him and he would be ill-prepared to cope with it. Of course, deep within his body good and necessary things would be happening. But since he had never fasted before he would feel terrible. Fasting takes time to get used to. This man's "extra" would be in useless fat tissues. After twenty days, he would no doubt be dragging, if not sick, and it would probably take him up to a month to regain full strength once again.

Look at the effect of the same fast on the other man, however. His body is in shape, finely tuned. It operates efficiently. He has fasted before. His body has learned to do without; it is well able to handle the temporary absence of food. So the twenty-day fast is no shock to his system. After the fast he would undoubtedly be operating at something less than peak capacity, yet he would still be strong and in full control, both physically and mentally. In fact, by this time he would probably be caring for his companion.

Now if these men are Christians, there is an additional factor to consider. During the times when we well may be forced to fast, it will be the responsibility of God's children to minister to those about them. This will be impossible if the circumstances are devastating His children as well. In order to do the things God will have for us to do, we will have to function at peak capacity. Urgent needs will be present in the days to come. Satan's reign on earth will be coming to an end and he will be unleashing evil among men as never before. The earth will be a spiritual battlefield. We will be engaged in a war against the powers of Satan. Spiritual insight and maturity won't be enough; we will also need physical strength and endurance to stand against him. We will need to be experienced in the methods of fasting and vigilant prayer for God's power to flow mightily through us. Both the physical and the spiritual results of our present fasting will see their fulfillment during those times.

These sorts of conditions have already begun in parts of the world. Consider the case of Richard Wurmbrand, fourteen years in Communist prisons because of his faith. Had his physical constitution not been hardy and his faith strong, he would not be alive today. As it was he endured and was responsible for the lives and emotional sanity of many of his fellow prisoners as well.

Such are the kind of people God will need in increasing numbers in the years ahead. Fasting and wise eating, while no substitute for godly wisdom and a deep daily trust in the Lord, provide vital preparation for such times and circumstances. They not only get our bodies and spirits into shape; they also prepare us for actual realities we may someday face.

3

Exercise

Prepare Your Body as Unto the Lord

Physical conditioning is going to play an increasingly important role in our lives in the days to come. Eating well and fasting regularly promote health and body efficiency. But these will not get your tissues, muscles and organs into shape. They provide a good foundation; but to build endurance and strength, your body needs vigorous physical exercise.

"What difference could it possibly make," you may wonder, "whether I'm in shape or not? Do I have to be an athlete to be a useful Christian?"

No, you don't have to be an athlete at all. God is able to use us all whether we've ever done an athletic thing in our lives or not. We have laid the foundation for assuming that the times ahead of us are going to involve physical trials. It becomes easy in our present western environment to underestimate what this time will be like. Physically demanding requirements will be made of us. They will be hard to endure; the person who's "out of shape" will collapse under the pressure. The Children of Israel, in slavery for years, were physically a tough people. How else could they have survived forty rigorous years in the barren desert and then have the stamina to drive armies out before them as they entered the promised land? God strengthened them for hundreds of years to ready them for their entry into Canaan. He is now doing the same with Christians today. Much will be required of us, as it was them, in strength and stamina. The unprepared will become a burden to the rest and will be unable to minister as well.

And if one thing should stand out to the world as characteristic of God's people, it should be that of loving ministry. God's people are to minister, not be ministered unto. Such ministry will demand an untiring physical effort. Being in shape, with bodies strong and toned both internally and externally, is not an option for Christians in the days ahead. It is an intrinsic part of our stewardship, our witness, and our ministry to others as we prepare for the difficult times that are approaching.

If you've never been part of a physical training program, you may wonder at this point how to strengthen your body and get it into shape. There is only one way—exercise!

It Must Be Strenuous

Nearly any form of vigorous exercise will strengthen your body and increase your stamina. But it must be just that—vigorous—to accomplish any permanent good. Many have the mistaken notion that *anything* physical will do. But that is not true. There are certain specific criteria physical exercise must meet in order to get us into shape. Unless they are met, we may have a good time, we may even huff and puff, but our bodies will not become stronger as a result of our efforts.

The two major things exercise must accomplish are these: make the blood flow much faster than normal through our veins, and make the lungs expand and contract rapidly filling much fuller than usual with air each time. In other words, we must get tired (panting hard!) to exercise our lungs, and our heart must be pounding (at double its normal rate or more) to give it the exercise it needs and to cause our blood to flow rapidly. Without heaving lungs and pounding heart, exercise won't accomplish all it should.

Running and swimming, therefore, are the best for accomplishing these goals. Tennis, long and rapid walks, basketball, bicycling, and handball will help too. Anything that makes you feel tired and makes your heart pound is doing the job. Much of what you will be able to do will depend on your age and situation.

A third ingredient effective exercise must contain is time. A few deep breaths and being tired for five minutes isn't the exercise we're talking about. For rapid breathing and increased circulation to actually work changes in your system, they must continue regularly for prolonged periods of time. Don't make the mistake of thinking being "busy" from morning till night is sufficient. To build stamina and strength exercise must be vigorous, prolonged, and put a definite strain on you. It makes you tired!

This third criterion imposes a definite limitation on the number of activities which will qualify. I don't for a moment suggest you give up bowling, golf, ping-pong, volleyball, skating, badminton, and the like. They're perfectly good activities which can accomplish worthwhile things—give skills, self-confidence, fellowship with others—besides being fun in themselves. These are legitimate motives. But generally they will not accomplish the things that need doing in your body. These recreational activities should be in addition to what I would call your "exercise."

Following the birth of our third child my wife enrolled in a "Slender-Rama" course with a friend for a month. We both knew the exercises she did there wouldn't increase her stamina. She wasn't doing it for that reason. It helped her lose some weight which boosted her self-esteem, gave her an opportunity to get out of the house, was a good discipline, and she enjoyed it. It was worthwhile for these reasons. But these slenderizing "exercises" didn't take the place of her need for additional vigorous exercise.

There are a couple quick tests you can do to determine some preliminary things about your physical condition. The first is to take your pulse rate. The average for men is about 72, for women about 75 to 78. The lower your pulse (generally speaking) the stronger and more efficient your heart (it is doing more work with fewer pulses).

I have been running for many years and my normal pulse is in the mid-40's. There is one distance runner on record whose pulse was recorded below 30 beats per minute. Though it may not be a totally accurate, medical picture, your pulse gives a rough measure of the strength of your heart and circulatory system. After years of running, a heart (such as mine, for instance) is strong enough to do the same work in 45 beats as most do in 72 beats—60% stronger. Anyone who runs and exercises regularly will have a stronger-than-average heart.

Another test is to run a mile. A man under 60 whose body is in shape from regular training will usually be capable of running a mile in eight or nine minutes. Many men in their forties can run a mile in six or seven minutes. Though such times take some prior conditioning, I mention them to illustrate what you may expect to achieve once you begin to get in shape. Unless you were born with an unusual amount of inherent endurance, such times would be nearly impossible "cold," with no earlier training. That's what makes this such a good test—you can't fool the watch. Such a test also gives you a good starting reference point from which to work and improve. It is amazing what you'll be able to achieve with a little work.

My ex-track coach, now over 60, can run a mile in six minutes. I know of a dozen or more men in their thirties and forties (that run regularly) who can run at a six-minute mile pace for several miles. These are average men who have worked their bodies up to that level of performance over a long period of time. Women can train and see similar achievements; for an accurate comparison you should probably add about a minute to a man's mile time. Age is a factor, of course, but not an excuse for laziness. If a mile in fifteen minutes is your fastest, then for you to run a mile at that pace will probably do your body as much good as for another man to run a mile in six minutes. The time is not the primary thing, but the effort relative to yourself. I mention these times only to provide you some general starting guidelines.

Most people who have not exercised much or participated in athletics in school have the tendency to think of physical training as only for a certain "athletic" sort of person. If that is your view, I want to tell you of a friend of mine.

My friend never participated in any sports throughout all his schooling. He did not enjoy P.E. classes, and his main interest was music. He had eye-coordination problems, had suffered from severe asthma for several years when young, and by the time he was in college he was overweight as well.

Somehow I managed to interest him in running. He began by running a couple of miles once in a while. The first time we ran together I finished ten or fifteen minutes ahead of him for a run of less than thirty minutes. He was really out of shape! But he stuck to it and gradually began to improve. We began to run more and more together over measured courses we had around town. Eventually he went a full six miles with me.

Then we began to run for time. On the six-mile course I would give him a ten minute head-start. Then five minutes. Then we began to run it together and finally he could beat me probably 1/3 of the times we ran. We ran a half-marathon race (13 miles) together, and he still holds our "course record" over a nine-mile course through town.

This friend had no more inate ability than I did—or you or anyone else. *Anyone* can achieve remarkable levels when they set their minds and bodies to it—no matter what the background. Running is something anyone can improve in remarkably. The same is true for any physical exercise. Some people will be more naturally gifted in certain areas. But everyone can improve. And our only real competition is against ourselves.

What Exercise Accomplishes

Vigorous exercise does a number of beneficial things in your body. Any part of the body, by being exercised, becomes stronger. This is true of your muscles, your mind, your entire body. By being forced to pump harder and faster your heart is strengthened. It becomes a stronger muscle.

Every pump pushes blood a little faster because each pump becomes a stronger pump. In the process your heart, like the arm of a weight-lifter, becomes enlarged slightly, further increasing its ability to do more work more easily. The lower pulse rate (which is also a stronger pulse rate) is evidence of this. The person who runs consistently will rarely have heart trouble as long as he continues to exercise.

The lungs are affected in a similar way because of the work load exercise puts on them. The lungs are forced (from rapid, deep breathing) to fill up more completely with air. This stretches them to their limit each time you inhale and gradually their capacity is enlarged (a balloon becomes easier to blow up after the first time because it has been stretched). Since the lungs become larger and stronger, like the heart they are able to perform more work with less effort. Not only will your pulse gradually lower but your breathing rate will also lower because of the increasing strength of your lungs.

During exercise itself, the heaving lungs which are gasping for air pull oxygen into your body at a much faster rate. Therefore your body gets a richer blend of oxygen in the blood during exercise (which is one of your body's ways of compensating for the increased demands on it). This is beneficial to every part of your body, especially the brain, not just the heart and lungs. The entire circulatory system is made to work at maximum efficiency at such times. Increased circulation of the blood also helps to keep vital organs such as the liver and kidneys clean and flushed out.

But probably one of the most important benefits of vigorous exercise is what is accomplished in our capillary system. Our blood veins and arteries carry the blood to all the extremities of the body. But from these larger vessels, the blood is actually delivered to the individual cells and tissues by millions and millions of tiny capillaries. They are so tiny they can barely admit more than a few cells of blood through them at a time. Our bodies are said to contain over 100,000 miles of this fine tubing which supplies oxygen and nutrients to every part of the body. Hard to believe, isn't it? We *are* "fearfully and wonderfully" made.

As the heart beats it sends blood throughout the entire body. It must be strong indeed to get the blood to all our cells through this vast network of 100,000 miles of veins and capillaries. A weak heart will simply not have the strength with each pump to send the blood everyplace.

As a result, if there has been insufficient exercise, over a number of years, capillaries in the remote parts of the body will get insufficient blood passage through them and will eventually begin to close up and collapse. Of course we don't notice this because there are still so many of them working. The point is, however, that our bodies at this point are not working at peak efficiency and are in fact in the early stages of breaking down. The capillaries begin to close from sheer inactivity.

As this happens, no matter how well you may eat and how adequate the nutrients you put into your body, there are some parts of your body that simply won't receive what they need. There is no way for that nutrition to get to your cells once the capillaries are blocked.

In addition, new cells cannot be formed as readily nor old wastes removed as effectively since that too is done via the bloodstream. Leviticus 17:11 comes alive for us, "The life of the flesh is in the blood" (KJV).

Exercise can dramatically turn this slow process of deterioration around. By making the heart pump faster it forces the blood at an increased rate through our entire body—veins, arteries, and capillaries. As the blood enters the smallest of the capillaries it is pushing harder and will therefore eventually open vessels that may have been blocked or closed. Since the heart is strengthened, it continues to pump more vigorously even when we are no longer exercising. Therefore the process of pushing blood through the capillaries harder and faster continues on, even in our sleep.

Eventually our stronger heart will force blood into new areas and new capillaries will actually begin to be formed. Blood finds its way into every minute part of the body. Nutrients are delivered and wastes removed. It becomes obvious why fasting can have its full and most beneficial effect only in a body whose circulation and capillary system is fully open and operational.

Not only does such exercise increase the efficiency of our entire bodily system *now*, but it also protects against heart trouble, atherosclerosis, lung problems, liver and kidney disease, and high blood pressure in years to come. Exercise is the best health insurance available.

Training Guidelines

To achieve such remarkable results, however, let me recap: your exercise must be regular, prolonged and rigorous. Bowling, leisurely walks, lounging in a swimming pool, or an easy game of softball won't qualify. It must tire you, tax your system; you've got to sweat! And neither will a major effort of ten minutes once a week do the job.

To build lasting strength into your heart and lungs and legs and muscles there must be a sustained effort. If you are presently out of shape you should begin very slowly and work up to it. One of the best methods of starting an exercise program is walking. Your goal is to get the blood flowing and walking will do it. You don't need to begin by running three or four miles. Take your time and build up slowly. But keep in mind that walking is but the stepping stone to more strenuous forms of exercise.

Once you do begin to get in shape (unless you have a weak heart, in which case your doctor should be advising you), you'll not need to worry about pushing yourself too hard. The more demanding (within reason) the exercise the better. Jogging can be almost miraculous, even when you may have suffered from some physical problems in the past. In our area there is a jogging program for victims of heart attacks. This is now being recognized as one of the best ways such a person can regain the strength of his heart and prevent another attack.

Once you move beyond the preliminary walking stage, there are a number of activities which when done regularly will accomplish this endurance building—swimming, bicycling, tennis, handball, touch football. But there is a significant problem with most of these activities. They are social in nature. Rarely do we swim hard for thirty minutes, pushing ourselves the entire way. Usually we are having fun in the company of others in the pool. Tennis, handball, football, and other games are clearly social. They are games and therefore must involve others. And what makes these things usually ineffective as training activities is that the effort is not continuous. There are frequent breaks and pauses throughout. The exercise itself is valuable, but the manner in which we perform it isn't prolonged. Walking and bicycling are less social, but their difficulty comes from the fact that they aren't ordinarily strenuous enough to tax the heart. They don't make you tired enough! Bicycling certainly can, but it must be kept up for such a long period it often becomes impractical.

Running/jogging, therefore, stands in a class by itself as the best form of exercise. (If you can overcome some of the weaknesses in these other activities—if you *can* cycle for long enough, if you *can* swim continuously, if several sets of tennis *does* keep your heart pounding furiously—then these will work fine as well.)

To determine whether or not your exercise is satisfactorily demanding (whichever form of exercise you engage in), consider the following criteria.

Your resting pulse is probably between 65 and 80. It will not be straining your heart significantly to get it up to 90 or 100. To strengthen your heart you must get it pumping fast—at least 120 beats per minute or more. Then you must hold it at that level for fifteen to thirty minutes. That is the only way the heart muscle can grow stronger. (Remember, we're not talking about doing such a thing "cold." You must work up to this level.) Any exercise which can accomplish that—a pulse increased between 50% and 100% and maintained for 1/4 to 1/2 an hour—will help.

As you start off, a long flight of stairs or a brisk walk around the block may do this to you. There are people who huff and puff all day during their ordinary activities. But as your conditioning gradually improves, it will take more and more strenuous training to tax your heart properly. After a while, running will be the only thing that will get your pulse up to 120 or 130 because you'll be in so much better shape. Unless your heart has a history of being weak, don't worry about overloading it (if you've worked up to it wisely). Your heart is a remarkable piece of machinery; it can take the extra work. It will thank you for it!

Jogging and Running—The Most Effective Exercise

During a run, it is not unusual for my pulse to exceed 150—3 1/2 times its normal pace. Once you're in shape, don't be afraid to push yourself.

If you must run on concrete you will initially face the uncomfortable side effects of a hard surface—aches, pains, bruises. A beach, field, sawdust trail, park, or the beach are always more enjoyable places to run and are not so hard on your legs, feet, knees, and joints. But we are not all fortunate enough to have such places close by. That mustn't become an excuse for not running. In all forms of diligent exercise there will be dozens of little annoyances which will plague you and tempt you to quit. You simply must remember how small they are when compared with the tremendous good you are doing your lungs, muscles, and circulatory system.

If you are able to swim regularly and hard several times a week, you won't have to face these sorts of things. But for the majority of people, running (with all its aches and pains) is much more convenient. You may think for one reason or another that you are simply physically not able to start running. But don't be overly quick to put yourself in this category. There is a man in our area in his late sixties whose physician warned him several years ago that he was slowly killing himself. "Unless you start some kind of exercise program, quit smoking, and start taking better care of your body, you're going to be dead before your time," he warned.

The man took his doctor's advice and gave up his cigarettes and began to run. He had years and years to make up for and his conditioning came slowly. To begin with he ran as slowly as 15- and 18-minute miles, slower than most of us walk. But he kept at it. Now he runs daily and participates in a community race of six to eight miles once a month. He is lean and trim and looks exceptionally healthy.

A good standard to aim for is to do your workout three or four times a week for thirty (continuous) minutes. It may take six months or more for you to attain this. That's okay. The important thing is to get started.

C. S. Lovett says, "It is a matter of stewardship of the body to get that blood moving every day." In fact, Lovett's testimony and diligent effort to be a good steward over his body has so encouraged me I'd like to share it with you.

> About two and a half years ago, I went to my doctor for a routine checkup. He found my blood pressure too high. . . . "You preachers don't get enough exercise. You ought to get out and jog. That blood pressure would come right down if you did. And that roll of fat would disappear too."
>
> That did it.
>
> After some weeks of [walking about the neighborhood] . . . I began to jog a little. After some weeks of that I started riding my bicycle to a nearby high school where I could do laps about the quarter-mile track. A month later I was doing the mile in 10 minutes.
>
> I now go three miles every day except Sunday. I don't go very fast. I still run the mile in about nine or ten minutes. Sometimes I like to show off and do it in eight minutes. But speed is not important, circulation is. And circulation is best helped by prolonged work at a steady pace. It is better to go further slower, than to sprint a short distance. . . . Once I discovered that God expects me to *work* this body, jogging or walking [became] a matter of Christian obedience. I am the steward of this animal. The Lord expects me to take care of it.
>
> My doctor promised that jogging would add as much as ten years to my life. That pleased me greatly. It is my desire to serve the Lord Jesus as long as I can. We all want to give Him our best. But how can we serve Him apart from these bodies? We can't.

And the apostle Paul is thinking of that when he says, "Present your bodies unto the Lord as a living sacrifice . . . " (Romans 12:1). Getting them into shape and keeping them that way has to be a part of Christian obedience.

It takes me about thirty minutes to go the three miles. It's a great way to fellowship with the Lord. As we chug along together, I praise Him for His own precious blood that makes me whiter than snow. Then I also thank Him for the physical blood surging through my body, making the organs like new. I'm on the track by 7 A.M. It's clear then, and there's no one around to hear me go through my prayer list. I even shout praises to the Lord now and then. Yes, this is one Baptist preacher who really gets "turned on" for Christ.

In my imagination I visualize my heart pounding 175 beats per minute, sending blood through the capillaries and washing and nourishing every cell in my body . . . I picture the capillaries being forced open and visualize the perfect health of my animal. I think of the 10 million new red cells being created every second and the tremendous power available to heal any area of my body. It wasn't long ago that physiologists believed a man past forty should slow down and take it easy. Doctors now believe the opposite. Most of them, including the nation's leading heart specialists, now insist that vigorous exercise is not only permissible for older people, but also necessary. I am now 55 and gaining more vitality every day since I started jogging two and a half years ago.[19]

A side benefit for the Christian is what a regular exercise program can teach about diligence and discipline. No one can do anything that is painful (which exercise can be!) for long periods of time without making a firm commitment to it. Sticking with it requires prayerful diligence. Like many aspects of living as a Christian, it is impossible to rely on feelings. You've just got to go out and do it, faithfully and persistently.

When more areas of our lives can be obediently approached in such a manner, the further the scripture will be evidenced in our lives: we are a chosen race, a royal priesthood, a holy nation, a people set apart and dedicated (1 Pet. 2:5). Being a vital, energetic, robust people in to-day's world is unique. To become such is indeed to set ourselves apart. God needs a people set apart and holy in many areas. Physical discipline and training is, I believe, one of them.

Running these past fifteen years has taught me much about my life with the Lord as anything I have done. Running in the unpleasant conditions of cold, darkness, snow, fog, rain, hail, and wind has developed in me a mental and spiritual endurance as well as physical. I am thankful for the discipline because I recognize that my priorities are going to have to be so well ordered and solid that I will not be swept away by the things that come upon the world. I consider my present physical training as preparing me both mentally and physically for that time.

In summary then, our physical preparation for the days and years to come contains three aspects—wise eating, regular fasting, and vigorous exercise. All three must work together to keep our bodies and minds in top shape for the Lord's return. None of them can be left out if we expect to be in first class "fighting trim." As the time approaches they all become more and more important.

4

Discipline

We Must Stop the Drift in Our Lives

These principles we are going to look at here could well fit anyplace in this book. They are vital to our success in every area, not only with those physical things we have just been discussing, though there is a definite value in talking about discipline here because our wills are particularly weak and we are all prone to laziness when it comes to losing weight, exercising, fasting, or changing our eating habits.

We have all probably done them—*for a while*. Making a zealous start is not usually the problem. But somehow over the long haul, most of us don't have what it takes to really stick to a change in our habits forever. We lack discipline.

As we face the future and a drastically changing world, we can content ourselves to remain as we are or we can set out to achieve a godly and prepared state of mental and physical health. In assessing these two choices that are before us we must realize that, as comfortable as it is to keep things as they are, the status quo is gradually changing. The world is slowly drifting downhill. The accepted norms of today are further from the principles of God than they were ten years ago. If we make the choice to "stay put" just as we contentedly are at present (which we can do subconsciously by not making the alternate decision), we unknowingly settle into this "drift" which is taking the world further and further from God. For those of God's people who want to firmly adhere to His principles, prepare for His coming, and separate themselves from the world and the direction it is headed, there comes a time to stand up and say *"stop!"* to the drift of the norm, the status quo. We must lay claim to a unique way of approaching life—in every area. Christians have always had the responsibility of demonstrating the uniqueness of the life of Jesus—a loving and giving spirit, eager to serve, willing to forgive, living the fruits of the spirit. These must continue to be our goals.

But no longer can our uniqueness, the things that set us apart from the world, be confined to such visibly spiritual actions and attitudes. In the coming years the uniqueness of the Christian's life-style must come right down to the foods he eats, the clothes he wears, how he earns his money, and how his children behave in school. If the world's fashions, the world's supermarket industry, and the world's educational system exert a pull to make the Christian conform, he must resist. He must order his life differently than the world dictates even in these areas we might think of as having little to do with the spiritual. Paul said, "Do not be conformed to the world" (Rom. 12:2, RSV). I think this means more than exhibiting the fruits of the spirit when the world does not. It must mean to resist when the world says, "These are the clothes you should wear," or, "This is the type of food you should eat." Obeying that exhortation covers every aspect of life.

Not only is the world drifting downhill as the day of the Lord's return draws ever closer but the demands on strong Christians are increasing. Their strengths and capabilities need to be deeper and more far-reaching. The present spiritual leader may one day find himself in prison. If he is not physically strong his spiritual leadership will mean very little. His ministry will depend on both physical and spiritual assets. When those days come God's people will not be able to afford the luxury of being nominally strong, occasionally strong, or fearful. We will *have to be* strong and victorious in order to minister to a seriously troubled world and bring it hope and the love of Jesus. Total spiritual, mental, physical, and emotional stability will be required of us, a people set apart for our calling.

It is obviously simplistic to say that adhering to these few principles we are discussing in this book will make you a victorious Christian. There is certainly much more to the victorious Christian life than these things. Yet in a very real way they do provide concrete examples of ways Christians today can separate themselves from the world and thereby resist the drift that threatens to ensnare them. Even a small act of resistance now multiplies with time and has far-reaching effects in later years.

Therefore, while it is possible to go along with those all about us (eat as they eat, spend money as they spend money, pursue similar goals, raise our children as they do), to do so increases the likelihood that a certain weakness or irresolution will creep unseen into our lives. It will be a vulnerability which has come from lack of training in the discipline of resistance to the ways of the world. To ignore this is to deny ourselves one of our greatest opportunities to become prepared for the future.

In everything we've discussed up until now and will discuss later, the success is based on faithfully disciplining ourselves to separate from the world. We will never be able to succeed in fasting (except temporarily) or in establishing new eating habits (except temporarily) or in an exercise program (except temporarily) without this attitude toward our efforts.

Once one has accepted the importance of resisting the ways of the world, there is a piece of machinery that must be set in motion in order to succeed. It is something God placed inside every person as part of the constituent make-up but which must be "switched on" before it can produce results. And that is willpower, discipline. Because everything around is geared up for a different direction, a different purpose, the world will constantly be exerting a pull on the Christian, trying to squeeze him into its mold. It takes a concerted effort of the will to keep from being gradually swept back into the current of one's former ways.

Will and Decision

Often we Christians balk at the mention of willpower. Talk about setting our wills in motion to accomplish something often has the implication that we are moving ahead on our own without the Lord. That isn't necessarily true. There is a principle running throughout nearly every phase of life, especially the spiritual realm, that can be summarized like this: an idea (a dream, a vision, a project, a goal, a faith-picture) can be turned into reality by believing in its reality and then by acting on that belief.

Vision—belief—reality. That is the process. All created things go through these stages as they become reality. God created man in this manner (Gen. 1:26, 27, KJV): "Let us make man in our image" (God had a vision of man in His thoughts.) " . . . and let them have dominion over the fish of the sea, and over the fowl of the air, and over the cattle, and over all the earth." (God believed His vision of man so completely that even though man was still not yet created, He already visualized him subduing all the animals and the entire earth.) "So God created man in his own image." (The reality of God's vision and belief came into being.)

If I am going to make something—a bookshelf, a chair, a

table, a house—I first have to "see" it. Then I "believe." I say to myself, "Hey, I can make that." Then I "act." I go out and build it and make of my vision and belief a reality.

This principle works in all aspects of life, not just when making material things. If I want to write a book, go to college, achieve a medical breakthrough, witness to my neighbor, lose twenty pounds, save fifty dollars for a special gift for my wife, lower my mile time thirty seconds, see my city evangelized, or carry out a twenty-day fast, the process is exactly the same.

I must act on my belief to turn the vision into reality.

God instituted this principle; and He expects it to be used in all aspects of lives that are submitted to Him. Once He furnishes us with visions, dreams, goals, insights, and wisdom, He expects us to *act* on them. And the primary tool God has given us in order to make this principle work is our will, not our mind. A brilliant mind can just sit still, but the will is the boiler room of the mind. The will is the seat of an individual's power. The will is where energy is created and used and where accomplishments—big and small—are begun.

It is willpower, then, thoughtfully and diligently applied day after day, which is the key to working changes in our lives—willpower which is persistent, even stubborn, in keeping its eyes on the goal and does not rely on a sporadic enthusiasm, however fervent, for motivation. And the enormous power of the will is harnessed and set in motion by one small mental act we must perform for everything we set our mind to do—the act of decision.

But "small" does not imply inconsequential, for this act of decision provides the will with an incredible power. This is much different from making up one's mind concerning several alternatives. "Have you decided what to have for lunch?" That involves a choice, but not a decision (at least in the way we are using the word). The decision that unlocks the strength of the will is made firmly, slowly, thoughtfully and irrevocably—and then stuck to *no matter what*! It is absolute and binding. From the depths of your being you accept what you have decided as an unalterable decision, not looking back or even allowing yourself to consider the possibility that you won't carry it out. The very act of making the decision binds you to it.

Sticking with the decision is the key to whether or not it will release the power of the will. When we make such a decision and then apply our will to carry it out, the result (that which we have visualized) will happen. You can depend on it.

When I was running competitively in college, a friend one day chanced to mention to me that Ron Clarke (a great Australian runner, a world-record holder) had missed no days of training in over seven years. His comment sparked the thought in my mind, "If I really want to be a good runner, then I just have to decide to run every day—period!" In that moment, though I did not realize many of the implications of it, I made a decision: to miss no more days of training.

I cannot say that I have not missed a day since. But I did run every day without fail for a year and a half and later put together a string lasting over three years and over 6000 miles. During those many consecutive days of running (in many adverse conditions, often when I would rather have remained inside warm and comfortable), I learned about the strength of the will to accomplish a goal. Sticking to my resolve required an enormous commitment.

So will sticking to the decision to exercise, fast, eat better, or do any of the things we'll be discussing later. Willpower is the only way you'll be able to accomplish what you set out to do. Your will is strong enough to see that you achieve any level of results on which you decide.

Allow God to Use Your Willpower

An exciting corollary to this principle for the Christian is that it is God who gives us our ideas and visions and goals and provides the substance for our beliefs. So when the mighty energy of our will is channeled in the direction He chooses, wonderful things can happen. You don't have to be a Christian to see the results of such disciplined resolutions, but they can reach their complete and highest fulfillment only when the decision-making process and the application of the will is in line with God's leading.

That does not mean we should sit passively back and wait for God to act. We must apply ourselves diligently to the part He has given us to do. This allows God to do His part along with ours. Remember God's word to the Israelites upon entering Canaan, "Every place that the sole of your foot shall tread upon, that have I given unto you" (Josh. 1:3, KJV). Their steps (under God's guidance) came first, His provision followed.

Therefore if you want to see some of these things we are talking about become real in your own life, you must do more than simply pray, "Lord, help me to lose weight, get in shape, start swimming regularly, spend my money more carefully, and begin eating better." Praying the prayer is the place to begin. But by itself such a prayer won't accomplish a thing. You must make the decision to do these things. And then you must put less on your plate, buy healthful foods, stick to your budget, and get in the water to swim. When your first enthusiasm wanes and you get tired of these things, you must apply your willpower to keep going. It is natural to lose enthusiasm for anything after a while. There are many mornings when it takes every bit of willpower I possess to get out of bed, put on my shoes and trunks, and go out for a six-mile run.

The question isn't whether or not you're going to lose your initial spark of motivation. The question is what you are going to do when it happens—give in or apply your willpower? I find myself lamely trying to rationalize, "I had to stop to walk because I was tired . . . it's too inconvenient trying to find foods without additives . . . I broke the fast because I was starting to feel weak."

Whenever I start to think such things I know the problem is a simple one: my willpower isn't working. I must constantly remind myself of my resolve to become prepared in as many ways as possible for the time of the Lord's return. And I know that means making certain changes in my life and my habits which require down-to-earth determined willpower.

The foundation for all this, of course, must be the Lord leading and directing our efforts. We can't just go off on our own in any direction we choose. When He makes the necessity of doing these things vivid to us, our wills are there to bring them into being.

This is how Nehemiah approached the task God gave him. The Lord directed him to rebuild the wall around Jerusalem. Nehemiah didn't wait for the Lord to do the job. Once his way was clear he set himself to do it (decision). He planned out the job, drew diagrams, gave the people their orders, and then made sure they followed through (the determination of the will following up on the original decision).

In a sense it was a very unspiritual project, much like an exercise or eating program would be. It was hot and sweaty and laborious work, a purely physical job. Sore muscles, tired feet, thirst, bruised knuckles, and frustrations were all part of it. God had said, "Build the wall," and from that point on it was merely a task of obedience. Nehemiah did not have to go to the Lord every so often for a reaffirmation of that original command. When problems arose he would go to God for specific guidance. But beyond that his only responsibility was to see that the command was carried out.

And the wall was built.

God's part and our part go hand in hand. There is a tight and inseparable interplay between God's guidance and our actions. Though we make a decision to obey God's guidance and our will determines to carry it out, yet all the time it is He who has created our wills in the first place and endowed them with their power. God's guidance and our obedience work together or they don't work at all.

Decision and the application of the will to carry it out—disciplined, determined willpower day after day as the Lord directs—is what makes living as a victorious Christian possible. The will is the energy source which will enable you to carry out any of these things you decide to do.

PART IV

PREPARING FOR THE FUTURE FINANCIALLY

Christian and secular writers alike predict that drastic economic change, possibly even collapse, is coming to the world. Inflation, devalued money, scarcity of needed items, lack of trust in government, and unstable international currencies are all early warning signals of trouble ahead. Many non-Christians, even though they approach such matters from a different standpoint, have been taking steps to guard against economic ruin. In the coming years we in the family of God will be forced to deal with this as well.

Preparation of some sort in economic matters is a must for the prudent Christian. Again, it is a matter of stewardship, diligence, ministry, and wise foresight. As we have noted earlier, should the world economy collapse and find us ill-equipped to deal with new conditions, we will face the same misfortunes as millions of others in the world. We will therefore find it very difficult to provide for and minister to those people in desperate need. We will be caught in the crunch of the same needs ourselves.

There are only so many financial provisions we can make, however. We must not mistakenly think that beefing up our bank account will stave off economic ruin. Our dollars could well become worthless, our bank accounts be seized and our possessions confiscated. Merely "putting aside" money and possessions will not insure that we are left with anything.

No, our preparation must take a different form. While the world would try to accumulate wealth to ward off future want, we must increasingly lessen our involvement in and dependence on the world economic system. I do *not* mean that we should buy small plots of land and "move away" into the hills to support ourselves. Christians must remain as long as possible in the thick of the world situation where the people are. God's people are to be the "light of the world," "a city set on a hill" for all to see. We cannot escape our calling. But though we are "in" the world, our usefulness will be measured by our disengagement from it.

At first glance this sounds suspiciously like a contradiction. But look for a moment at Jesus. Do we not observe the supreme example of that very enigma in His life? Constantly surrounded, hounded, followed, questioned, beseiged by crowds, He nevertheless remained pure, calm. He lived *in* the world but was not *of* it. This should be our goal.

In these final days such a divorce from the *ways* of the world will affect us in very practical areas. In financial matters such a separation must force us to scrutinize closely our jobs, how we acquire money, our spending habits, and what we consider the nature of prosperity, as well as our entire outlook on money and how God is able to work in our lives as a result. Let's do some of that scrutiny in the next section.

1

Becoming Self-Supporting

Money Needn't Always Come from the World

We've already examined numerous ways of lessening our reliance on the world while remaining in it—growing food, using our hands skillfully, fasting so that food scarcity won't overwhelm us. However, most of us do remain hopelessly immeshed in society's economic system in one of the most important areas of our provision—our jobs. For the majority of us the money we need to live comes through business and governmental institutions. If our only means of support is a check from the state, the corporation, the school, the store, or the mill we will discover that we are at the mercy of these organizations once times become more severe and money becomes tight. When we find ourselves with little money to support our families, we will be incapable of ministering to others as we should. Since our supply is the world, when that source stops we will be dependent on it more than ever.

That we use the world's money, however, does not necessarily mean we must depend on the world to supply it. It is possible to make money on your own. Today's economy, in spite of its vulnerability, nevertheless remains filled with opportunities for the person who is trained to see them. It is entirely feasible to carve an income out of the economy without having to rely solely on others.

This can be exciting for Christians anticipating the future. Though we admit, "There is surely collapse coming and these opportunities which presently exist are temporary," yet at the same time we can say, "But until that happens I can adequately support myself and my family with my hands, abilities, and knowledge and at the same time will lessen my involvement with the world. When collapse does come, it will not devastate us." Money can be made in our western democracy. To do so is simply a matter of discovering where the openings exist and then training ourselves to take advantage of them (buy the goods, make the products, sell our talents, etc.).

Christians can be self-supporting. There are a multitude of ways this can be accomplished: starting your own business so that you are responsible for your own opportunities; earning a living with your hands (plumbing, carpentry, gardening, painting, roofing, sewing, repairing cars, manufacturing things to sell—there are countless ways to use your ingenuity and physical skills); being a skilled professional such as a doctor, dentist, counselor, real estate or insurance agent, accountant or lawyer—unlimited variety to all the potential ways for making money. Since money is necessary for us to survive at present, why not then create our own flow rather than depending on outside sources for it?

Of course when economic pressures reach a certain point, self-supporting Christians will be affected as well as everyone else. But by creating our own financial sustenance in *practical* ways, there will be an increased freedom for us to seize upon a wider range of opportunities, even after that deterioration begins. Our capacity to minister to those who are suffering from the effects of the crumbling economy will be greatly prolonged.

One of the principal means of insuring that our self-supportive methods will be able to endure is to choose them on the basis of their practicality and universal need. Those who earn their living by supplying a common need are supporting themselves in the most practical way of all. Being in business for yourself won't necessarily help you later on if you are selling an item or a skill or a professional service for which there will be little demand once the economy begins to slide downhill. Being a doctor or selling food is clearly more practical than being a lawyer or selling pleasure boats.

Practicality is important for another reason—ministry. When eventually the financial aspects of our self-supporting jobs decline, we will be left with only the skills, insight wisdom, connections, sources of supply, and abilities we have gained through the process. And when these skills, etc., are usable and practical, our work will be able to continue on uninterrupted as ministry, even though there may be no money to show for it.

Christians will function as a community. One man is a doctor, another a mechanic, another a builder, another a dairy farmer, another a baker, another a vegetable gardener, another a fabric manufacturer. These men all have skills and products the others need. They will be able to support each other. Among Christians in those days, it is possible that money will be scarcely necessary.

Self-sufficiency in our vocation, therefore, enables several things to happen. It enables us to live in freedom from a total dependence on the world and its systems. We gain skills and talents and knowledge and experiences that enable us to capitalize on opportunities we could not otherwise use. We are able to minister to those in need by making use of our skills. And we will later be able to productively function within God's body in such a way that the entire Christian community is able to sustain itself. All her talents, wisdom, and possessions will blend together into a working whole.

How It Could Work—Things to Consider

Rarely will vocations easily fall into clear categories—practical, unpractical, self-supporting, dependent on the world. Most situations will have a mixture of several of these elements. We must learn to evaluate occupations, skills and interests from a number of different angles to determine potential pros and cons.

Take my own profession, for example. I am in the business of selling books. I am aware that in one sense books are a luxury item which people will not buy when they barely have enough money to sustain life itself. From that standpoint, then, mine is an impractical profession.

But mine is a Christian bookstore. We sell Bibles and related teaching aids that are going to be increasingly needed in the days to come. Imagine a Christian community with no source of supply for Bibles? Christians need God's Word. Therefore I perceive that the ministry of the Christian bookstore will be crucial in the days to come, even if someday our store is forced to go "underground" to distribute Christian literature. (God's Word is not only scarce but outlawed already in much of the world and it seems certain this trend will continue.) This is the side of my vocation that I feel is practical and highly preparatory for what is coming.

Consider the auto mechanic. Even though he works for some company now and is not in a strict sense self-supporting, he nevertheless earns his living with his hands. His is a very practical profession. As long as cars and trucks and tractors and rototillers and lawnmowers and all sorts of machinery continue to be used, his skills will be of great value to the rest of God's people.

The Christian who is a doctor is in a position with wide flexibility. For he is able to be self-supporting now; and as the conditions in the world grow worse and worse, his training and skills will be even more valuable. Physical needs multiply during difficult times, and doctors will undoubtedly be among the busiest people on earth during the coming tribulation. Think of it—a Christian man of God saving the life of another and then being able to say to him, "The power of God has healed you!"

Or take the Christian grocer who over the years establishes business contacts with other Christians. He buys fresh vegetables from one man, fruit from another, dairy products from another, and buys his meat from a Christian in a nearby community who operates a slaughterhouse.

The time may come when this man's business license will be revoked and his store evacuated from its premises. But the years have taught this grocer that the success of his operation is not dependent on his prime location, his glass cases, and his well-stocked shelves. He has learned to look to the Lord to supply his need. So rather than becoming despondent over the turn of events, he begins to put his knowledge, his background, his experiences, and the connections he has built up to work in finding ways to make food available to other Christians and to those in desperate need. I can't think specifically of how he would accomplish this. But I do know that as he relies on the Lord both to supply his own need and to open the doors to ministry, his preparation and continued obedience to God would become a significant part of the Christian community in which he was a part.

What could be more practical than the skills of the handyman? A carpenter is an excellent example—the man who can support his family at present by building will be an invaluable asset among God's people later. The plumber, the all-around-fix-it man, the seamstress will all be in great demand in future years.

What about the Christian farmer? Perhaps his is the most practical and important position of all. Should Christians eventually be persecuted to the extent that they are *forced* out of the cities onto plots of "community" land, the man who knows how to make the land yield rich harvests will be mightily used of God.

The teacher is in one sense in an impractical position because he is ordinarily dependent on the governmental system for his livelihood. Yet on the other hand, teaching is a necessary and vital aspect of training in God's body—both teaching of young children as well as spiritual teaching of principles and skills to adults. Teaching, therefore, becomes a difficult profession to analyze. Christians are needed as never before in school systems to influence and mold young lives in positive directions. Yet because of the institutional dependence, the Christian teacher is wise to think of a secondary, more practical, vocation with which he can supplement his teaching should conditions one day force him to do so.

What about self-owned Christian businesses? It would depend of course on the specifics of the business. Selling expensive imported furniture is in a different class than selling clothes, fresh produce or shoes. But in most businesses, as in mine, there is a mixture of many factors. One of these considerations is the future availability of the products which he must purchase from large companies elsewhere—auto parts, books, clothing, furniture, equipment, hardware, and so on. Being in business for yourself is of no value if you have nothing to sell.

For the enterprising Christian, it is possible to gain great business wisdom and, in a sense, to create your own availability. Some future-minded businessmen could seek out Christian manufacturing outlets or could sell clothes, simple furniture, household items, and so on, that were made locally. I have asked myself these questions in connection with our book business. "Should we consider a small-scale publishing operation to complement our bookstore, so that when literature from our major suppliers becomes unavailable we could print it ourselves?" I would encourage Christian businessmen whenever possible to deal as much as they can with other Christians. It cannot always be done exclusively. But the more Christians support one another's various enterprises, the more solid they will continue to be, despite troubled times.

These are but a few examples. There are a host of professions, skills, and businesses God will be able to greatly use. Thoughtfully and prayerfully and creatively think through your own personal options in light of all considerations.

Prepare Right Now—Acquire Practical Knowledge and Skills

Much of your vocational preparation will depend on where you are right now. If you are just entering college and are seeking the Lord about which direction your life should go, a multitude of options are open to you. If, on the other hand, you have a family and a good job which you have been involved in for twenty years, your options will be much more limited.

The point isn't that we should suddenly bail out of our present situations in order to become self-supporting. For those who have a stable job and who therefore face no urgent need to support themselves, the goal should simply become: acquire the capacity to be self-supporting, learn practical skills. This should be a goal for all of us, no matter what our current situation. By becoming familiar with a wide range of practical things you become a much more useful person—to God, yourself, your family, and others—both now and in the future. A paying job isn't the necessary criteria for the usefulness of a skill. Even if you never do use an acquired skill to earn an income, having it will be advantageous. It will mean one more area of service you are able to offer others, and it will be one additional ability you could turn to should your job one day become extinct. The acquiring of practical abilities is always beneficial.

Once you are exploring some areas of interest, you should look for every opportunity to practice the abilities you are learning. Practice them as a hobby or by helping others. Discover all the ways you can to put your growing talents to work, whether they are physical, organizational, or managerial. You must use the talents God has given you or they will wither.

For many, probably the majority, such an expanding range of capabilities will remain for years as a method for service—sharing what God has given in your spare time. Its potential as a self-supporting money-making occupation will lay dormant as long as your present job lasts.

Others, however, whose extra-vocational skills are fairly solid will begin to consider the possibility of eventually working toward a self-supporting state. If you are one of those, the first step for you might be to ask yourself whether you might be able to supplement your present income by practicing your skills on the side. It is not necessary to jump in completely all at once. Taking on small side jobs could be an indication of how successful you could be at it eventually full time. You should be constantly evaluating your skills and abilities and training yourself in every way you can. This might mean saving some money, taking a training class, working evenings or weekends to master new techniques and seeking out experts to learn from. And the underlying mind-set should be the important aspect of God's being able to use these new skills He is giving you for the benefit of others. Long before you actually branch out on your own you should be ministering with the resources He has provided. If you never do become fully self-supporting as a result, nevertheless you have learned some valuable things that will enable you to help others.

The time may come at some point when you feel confident that you could sustain yourself on the basis of your work that has up till now been merely a sideline. As your opportunities continue to build so that it becomes nearly impossible to carry on your regular job in addition to the side work God is providing, then possibly the time is approaching when you should consider making a small-scale self-supporting business out of it.

Wise thought and prayer are vital when making decisions like this. The guidance of the Lord must be clear. Launching out on your own contains many hidden risks and expenses. Especially if you are supporting a family, such a decision must come slowly. Branching out into making a living on your own in today's economy is a risky proposition. God will bless and honor your efforts, but He will not keep you out of hot water if you are foolish. Sound business principles must be followed to succeed. It is estimated that less than 20% of new businesses succeed. So the odds are against you as you begin to support yourself. Therefore use caution, wisdom and care in what you do.

The majority, however, will not be led to leave their current positions to support themselves. This does not mean they have no responsibility to prepare as well. They should be learning useful, practical skills that they can use not only to help people but that also contain the potential of a secondary or back-up occupation should they some day need one. Even if we have no intention of quitting our job as long as it lasts, we must be aware that a different day is coming. We can lay the foundational groundwork for that time by working toward self-sustaining skills and knowledge in our spare time. As we are preparing in this manner, a crucial factor is that we learn competence in areas as independent as possible from the world economy. Though we do not need necessarily to be independent now, because the world is able to help sustain us at present, there should be built into our skills the potential to continue on even if the world market does not.

Being independent from the world does not always imply owning your own business or working with your hands. There are many, many ways God can work toward the total self-sufficiency of His people as a whole without each individual being totally independent. We are a body and all the parts fit together. For instance, if you are working for a Christian, you can evaluate your position much differently. I have several excellent employees in my bookstores. I hope they never have to leave the ministry of our store because we all share together the vision of what we are trying to accomplish through its various facets. We are a team. These people are not self-supporting as such, yet they are in positions that are independent of the world and that should continue on despite the world's economy.

Your particular gifts and abilities may not be physical at all. God did not endow everyone with equal manual dexterity. The talents of some lie in administrative areas. Yet there are still ways to contribute to the sustenance of God's people apart from the world. God will provide many of His people with very good-paying jobs and prosperous businesses. It may be the responsibility of such Christians to put their financial resources, rather than their hands, to work. Money at present creates opportunities and God is able to use it wonderfully in the right hands. My father invested heavily in my business to help get it going. In this particular case, he has put his resources, rather than his hands, to work for the Lord in practical ways.

In summation, as Christians facing the future in an uncertain world, it is our responsibility to prepare by lessening our dependence on the world for our supply—things, money, services, and so on. The more Christians are capable of providing for themselves as a body, the less the decay of the world about them will undermine their capacity to minister to those in need. We can all begin to work toward this state of godly self-sufficiency right now by beginning to develop the practical talents, skills, interests and knowledge God has given us. In some cases this will mean Christians operating self-supporting businesses; in some cases it will mean Christians using resources God has made available to them to create opportunities for others. But for all of us, no matter what our position, age, present vocation or interests, it means seeking ways to develop those areas of knowledge and ability God has given us. While not necessarily taking us out of the world at present, such practice increases our usefulness to the rest of God's body and also prepares us for the eventual time when we may be required to depend less and less on the world economy for our sustenance.

Examples of Some Who Have Followed These Principles

These principles are not merely theoretical. They have been followed by many who are now using their skills and resources in practical ways—some to support themselves, some to supplement their existing income, and some to minister with no thought of financial gain. To provide you with a clearer picture of ways these ideas can be implemented I'll share with you several illustrations.

My own Christian bookstore began the year after I finished college while I was teaching. For the entire first year, putting a few shelves of books in my apartment was more of a part-time hobby than a business. Even when the store began to grow rapidly, both my wife and I continued to teach part time to help support it. Eventually, when it became clear the store was going to be able to support us permanently, we threw ourselves into it completely. (This growth is detailed in my book *Growth of a Vision.*)

I've already mentioned my father's part in that process. He provides another example of financial independence as well. In the early years of his own career, my dad learned the basics of house-wiring. It had nothing to do with his job; he simply picked it up over a period of time. After a while he had become a rather expert electrician and could easily have been a professional. This was a case of his having a "back-up" practical vocation should the need ever have arisen. It never has, however, and his electrical proficiency has remained a means of his helping others with wiring problems rather than something he has done for pay. I do not remember his ever accepting money for his services. But he completely wired many, many houses and helped countless people with minor electrical tasks.

There was a man in our church I had known for years who worked in management for a large lumber corporation. He had no business experience from a retail sales perspective. Yet he availed himself of every opportunity to learn as many different aspects of business as he could. He gained much practical experience in dealing with the public. In his spare time over the years he also trained himself to work with his hands to a high degree of proficiency. He learned to use many types of power tools, to wire electrical connections and understand the circuitry involved, and to do many kinds of woodworking jobs.

Then suddenly, after many years with the firm and with only ten years to go until his pension, his job was phased out of the company's operation.

What could he do? It was obviously too late in life to make a brand new start in an altogether new career. But this man had been preparing all his life. He had abilities and had gained insights over the years that could actually help support him (though he hadn't been aware of this preparatory process going on). He provides the perfect illustration of the need to prepare practically for the future, whatever happens and whenever it happens.

To shorten the story, this man and I got together and began talking about some goals I'd been thinking about as well as about his uncertain future, and within four months he was managing a brand-new branch of our store. All the skills and knowledge he had acquired through the years were superb training and background. Within weeks he had picked up the entire operation like an expert! Had I found it necessary to teach him from scratch it would have taken years. But his self-training over the years, in *practical* areas, completely took the place of that necessity. Ordering, advertising, building fixtures, installing lights, handling money, making repairs, and managing employees came naturally to him because he had trained himself in such a wide variety of areas, acquiring useful and practical skills and knowledge.

This is the sort of "preparedness" that will make us more useful and ministering Christians in the days ahead.

I have a very close friend who, along with myself, trained to become a teacher. But after a year in the classroom it became obvious to him that he could never be completely contented there. He wanted to be on his own, to work with his hands. So after that first year he quit teaching and began to study for his building contractor's license. He studied nights, weekends—whenever he could squeeze in the time. In the meantime he took a job with another contractor. Within three years he had moved up and could look forward to a bright future with this company, complete with retirement benefits and good pay.

Yet still he wanted to be on his own. Eventually he took and passed his contractor's exam and quit a secure job for a second time, this time to go it alone. For a time it was very hard financially for his young family. But he has now completed two very high-quality homes; and because of the valuable experience he has gained, he has almost more job offers than he can handle.

A similar series of events happened to another man with whom I went to school. He was an electrical wizard, working for an electronics firm. On the side he was constantly busy fixing some piece of equipment for someone he knew. This avocation continued to mount until it began to infringe on his regular job. Gradually he was forced to take more and more time off just to keep up with it.

Realizing his dilemma, he began to establish some rates and fees and to make of his spare-time work a small-scale business. He didn't quit his job immediately, but gradually the one was growing while the other was diminishing.

Finally the time came when he was able to quit his job and go into his repair business full time. There were, of course, risks. There always are when you are working for yourself. His income is not as predictable as it was before. But he is on his own and can look to his own efforts to make it grow.

I have another friend who visualized a business which would merchandise clothing by equipping Christian women with material and supplies to make them in their own homes—a perfect example of what we have been discussing. Shirts, blouses, and so on, are practical items that everyone needs. Since they are made in private homes, overhead is minimal. As long as the market for such items continues in the world, they can be profitably sold in stores throughout the country. Yet if that market begins to dry up, imagine the potential in having the facilities already established to produce clothing for Christians in need?

Using your resources for the benefit of others does not

necessarily mean giving away your possessions and doing things for free. The Scriptures teach us that the servant is worthy of his hire. And that earned money can be used to support Christian endeavors.

There is a man in our church whose God-given talents were more in the area of administrative ability. He had taught for some years in the public school system, had helped to begin a small experimental school, and authored a state educational textbook. When he became a Christian God gave him a vision for opening a Christian school in our area. At first it was largely a one-man project; the odds against its success were heavy. There was no money, no location, not sufficient time, and no experienced teachers. But his vision was strong. He knew it could happen so he kept at it.

And the school was opened. The classrooms were in the educational unit of our church. The teachers were Christians and much of the help was voluntary. The first year was a struggle. But the school survived. The second year was better and bigger. Now, after four years, the school is on a solid foundation. It is not dependent on federal funds in any way and is therefore independent and self-supporting in the manner we have been discussing. The children are getting solid, biblical teaching. There are enormous benefits from every perspective. This is a living example of bringing faith-pictures into reality (as discussed in the last chapter) as well as a way in which the Christian community can support itself and become sustaining apart from the world's system.

"Self-supporting" does not necessarily mean that one goes into business. In this particular case, my friend is not self-supporting in a strict sense. He receives his salary from the school organization. But he has helped bring into being an entire school which is not dependent on the world in any way. The children are from Christian homes and the tuition the school receives is from Christian people. The local church body is educating its own children and is financing the process itself.

From these few examples and from numerous others with which you are undoubtedly familiar, it can clearly be seen that there are no quick and simple formulas which will fit us all. No one can say, "*This* is precisely what you should do to prepare for the future vocationally." The Lord's guidance must be in every step we take, as well as a keen awareness of the responsibility to our family.

But some general guidelines should by now be apparent. Most important among them is that we all should be developing the interests, skills, and talents God has given us, seeking especially practical ways to practice them for the benefit of others. In so doing we fulfill several scriptures (Matt. 25:20; Prov. 12:24; 12:27; 1 Cor. 7:7; 1 Pet. 4:7-11). We are able to minister and arm ourselves practically for the day when we may have to turn to the labor of our own hands to sustain the needs of life.

2

Financial Prudence and Prosperity

Control of Money—A Key to Increasing Responsibility

It may seem there is a certain inconsistency in having said earlier, "The economy is sure to collapse and our monetary system along with it," and now turn to the discussion of money and prosperity as if the earlier statement were to be disregarded. Let me assure you, however, of the continuing importance in knowing where our economic system is headed. But this does not mean we can disregard the role of money in our lives. Though money as we presently know it may be temporary, nevertheless, to live and function and serve effectively in the world presently requires that we have money and use it wisely for God's glory. Financial stewardship, therefore, is a must for every serious Christian, especially those who evaluate the present with a careful eye also atuned toward the future. Though the use of money itself may be temporary, gaining wisdom in financial matters develops and deepens qualities within us—diligence, responsibility, unselfishness, discretion, purity, and trust—which will continue to be part of our spiritual selves long after money itself ceases to exist.

Money occupies an almost contradictory place in the minds of many Christians. Because we are so often reminded that the love of money is the root of all evil, it is easy for us to view prosperity as something we should shun. The problem is that we have a difficult time distinguishing between money itself and the love of money.

We do well to be very careful in our thinking about money. It can be a very subtle yet strong temptation toward the world. Unless you are strong enough in the Lord to resist, Satan can indeed grip you with a love of money and quickly pull you away from following the principles of God.

Money itself is not an evil thing. It is a strong and powerful tool and much care needs to be taken when handling it. Money is much like a wild stallion. If you are weak and unable to remain in control, it will trample and kill or maim you. Yet on the other hand, if you *are* strong enough to master it, tame it, stay in the saddle, and control it skillfully without allowing it to gain mastery over you, then you have harnessed a great and powerful force. God can make great things happen when that strength is tamed and brought into line with His purposes.

In today's economy, though it may be fleeting, money is indeed a powerful tool. God has things He wants to do. He does not ignore any tool that can be used to spread His kingdom, including money. But if things are going to happen with money, the first thing we must do is learn to control it.

The first step toward our being able to effectively do that is to gain control. This means far more than just establishing a budget for a few months. It is a long, long process that can take years. We must guard our attitudes toward money and keep it out of the world's grooves. The scripture, "He who is faithful over little will be given responsibility over much . . . and to him who is not faithful over little, even what he does have will be taken away" (Matt. 25:23,

29—author's paraphrase), is rarely so apt as it is concerning money matters.

Because of the frailty of human nature, the risk involved in giving us something so potentially devastating as a great amount of money means that God must train us in the area of little things before giving us greater financial responsibility. This could be why so many struggle continually to make ends meet. God knows the danger of having too much money. So He provides us with just what we need, with only a little to spare. He then observes our reactions: how thankful we are for His provision, how we handle it, and whether or not we are learning to do so wisely and unselfishly. The more wisdom we learn to exhibit with what He provides (however small the amount) the more He is able gradually to increase the supply.

The point isn't that God wants to make us all rich. Money is but one aspect of prosperity. He is trying to teach us wise judgment and discernment in all areas of our lives. God must have control of all phases of your life, and your finances are an integral part. As we see in the parable of the talents (Matt. 25:14-30), He can use our everyday experiences in money handling to prepare us for further responsibility. If you are one who is barely squeaking by financially, I would encourage you to take a long, hard look at your situation. Try to visualize it from God's point of view. Ask yourself, "Is my wise financial stewardship opening up the possibility for God to entrust me with further 'talents'?" If this is not the description of your present situation, possibly the basic guidelines in the next section will be of help and encouragement.

Though many of God's specific plans for us all may differ, His universal desire is to bless His people. God *wants* to bless you. God especially wants you to know the joy of trusting Him rather than your checkbook for meeting all your needs. According to the trust you exhibit in His supply, the thankfulness of your heart for His provision and the faithfulness you show with the amount He presently has given you, He will bless you. And as your money increases, so will your capacity to minister to others.

Guidelines for Wise Spending

There are some very basic principles that are absolutely essential if you want to learn wise money management. As in all aspects of your spiritual walk, *knowing* these principles will do you little good; you must faithfully and regularly *practice* them. We have all seen people who flit from one new book to another, from one exciting principle to another, and from one spectacular meeting to another but whose daily lives remain stagnant, without any noticeable changes. This results when one does not put the principles to work. Many of the things in this chapter won't be much fun to practice. We'd all prefer just to ignore much of this. Nevertheless, our faithfulness here will have widespread implications in other areas of our lives.

If you want God to bless you financially with the means to provide comfortably for your family and also minister to others, it is vital that God see your stewardship in action—the judicious management of your money *right now*.

Everything we have belongs to God.

Principle number one is the foundation for all the others. He gives material and financial blessings to be *used*, but a Christian does not actually *own* them. "You possess, but God owns." [20] This may sound simplistic, even trite. But unless this is clear in your mind, you can get into great bondage over money. It may not happen tomorrow, but in order to keep a balanced perspective on money, we need to remind ourselves daily that all we are and have belongs to God.

There are two tithes.

Once we have the first principle in order, we are ready to put more specific ideas to work in the daily budget. Yes, there are two tithes—a tithe to God and one to yourself. You already know about tithing (traditionally 10% but actually according to the Old Testament probably above 20%), a scriptural amount given to God (Lev. 27:30). The second tithe, like the first, should be taken off the top. This is one of the secrets of financial prosperity and ministry—having an amount saved. It might be in a savings account for a specific goal—a down payment on a house, for a new car, for unexpected medical expenses. Or you might use it to help someone in need. But in order to be able to use it you must first have put it aside. And it will not grow into a usable amount unless you do it regularly.

But don't make the serious error of saving simply to accumulate wealth. "Those who want to get rich fall into temptation and a snare and many foolish and harmful desires which plunge men into ruin and destruction" (1 Tim. 6:9, NAS). Save with a purpose that is submitted to God's will—for extra giving, to buy with cash rather than being forced to use credit, for a family investment, for someone's need.

You may be presently living on such a minimal amount you can't imagine putting aside 20% before taxes! It may take some practice and certainly some working up to (just because you aren't able to save 10% doesn't mean you can't start with 1% or 2%—the totals will add up faster than you think), but after you begin to apply the rest of these financial principles I think you'll find it's easier than you think. A couple we know (whom I'll tell you more about later) managed to save 40% of their income over a year and a half period under near-emergency conditions. It *can* be done.

Such a savings and giving plan takes serious commitment and a great deal of self-control. There is only one way to give more and save more. And that is to spend less. There are no gimmicks. Just like losing weight, you can try all the programs, read all the books, and enroll in all the courses you want to; but when it comes to the bottom line, to lose weight you have to eat less. And to save and give more, you have to spend less. There's only one way to do this—self-control and self-discipline.

If you want to achieve financial freedom and be given greater responsibility by God, you must take tight, ruthless control over your spending. Here are some ways to do it.

Buy Only Necessities

Before every purchase, ask yourself three questions:

1) Can we afford it?
2) Do we *really* need it?
3) Would it be possible to live without it?

You'll quickly discover you can live without many things.

Never Buy Impulsively

Great wisdom often comes with the passage of time. If a great deal comes along that "can't wait," it's probably not as good a deal as it seems. Think out every purchase. At the supermarket or the discount drugstore an almost unbelievable number of purchases are made impulsively, just because something that strikes one's momentary fancy is seen. By eliminating such indescriminate buying you will achieve results in a hurry. Be merciless when answering question number three.

Never Buy on Credit

If you think you must charge something, you probably don't need it immediately. Credit buying is devastating to a budget for two very significant reasons. In most cases, when you buy on time, you wind up paying almost double the original price (if the payments are strung out over a long period, which they usually are). And in addition, credit offers lure you into buying things you wouldn't otherwise— things you don't really need, don't have the money for and could just as well do without.

Scrutinize Before Buying

When we spend money with wisdom and intelligence, we don't always have to have the top-of-the-line models. If you need a new refrigerator, you can spend $1200 or you can spend only $150 (for a perfectly good used one). If your financial situation is tight, charging a new, expensive unit with a host of "features" won't be worth the long-range debt.

On the other hand, discretion is very necessary here. I

have a friend who is so tight with his money he buys nothing but junkers for transportation. Over a four-year period he spent more money on various questionable "deals" and subsequent maintenance than I spent by simply investing in a solid automobile that cost me considerably more initially. You do not always save by buying the cheapest. Find the balance in light of your means.

Learn to "shop," not buy. We are all experts at spending money. But learn to hunt out good bargains. Read consumer magazines, visit various stores, check catalog prices, look for sales, talk to people. Don't buy (especially something major) without first having methodically considered every detail on all available models.

Don't buy something just because it is on sale. If you are going to buy something *anyway*, then of course wait until it is marked down whenever you can. But to always think a sale means savings is deceiving. We have a friend who, when she was pregnant, excitedly told us about finding $50 worth of baby clothes on sale for $15. She was so pleased to have "saved" $35. The clothes, however, were of the grab bag sort and many of them obviously would never be used. I could not help but question the "savings." There would have been a much simpler way for her to genuinely save $15 and wind up with the cash actually in her pocket—not buy the clothes!

You do not save by spending. You save by NOT spending.

Don't Waste Money

This may sound obvious. "Who would ever do such a thing?" you may wonder. But we all do whenever we spend foolishly and don't take proper care of what we do have.

When we properly care for the things we have, the longer it will be before we'll have to replace them. Let's not get caught up in the fashion trap. What could possibly eat up money faster than trying to keep "in style"? Clothes have a function. When they wear out and no longer perform that service, then it is time for new ones. But until then you do not need a constantly increasing and changing wardrobe.

Similarly, what can exhaust your funds quicker than giving it to a beauty shop for hair styling, a drugstore for cosmetics and perfume, or a jeweler for a new necklace. Our society offers countless ways to squander our money and have little to show for it: eating out regularly, buying expensive furniture, accumulating gadgets with limited use but great appeal, spending for exotic toys. We should have something to show for the majority of our purchases—something useful that does not merely collect dust after its newness wears off. We all are highly susceptible and TV advertising *assaults* us where we are most vulnerable.

Avoiding waste does not necessarily imply never buying anything but absolute essentials for life itself. God does allow some latitude. But when we come to the place where we can consider a few luxuries, we must be guided by whether we can afford them without affecting our two tithes or our other giving. Our purchases must accomplish something, be part of a goal.

Curb Appetites

What all this boils down to is curtailing all your appetites—saying *no* to your wants, desires, and self-indulgent past, then leaving your billfold or checkbook in your pocket and walking on by. It takes enormous self-discipline and you will not succeed without having made a major decision to do so.

This probably sounds rather harsh and cold, but God wants merciless control exhibited over our money. Once that pattern has been established He will then be able to move us on into wider ranges of responsibility. May I remind you that He wants us practiced and ready for whatever comes to the world.

Set Limits and Stick to Them

This is what budgeting is all about: making yourself adhere to a pre-determined amount of money. There are many excellent books which you should read on how to establish a budget if you are unfamiliar with the procedure. But as with anything, a budget will not work unless you rigorously decided that you *will* stay under the amounts you have established. Budgeting does not mean determining how much you want to spend in a given area, writing it down, and then spending that much. Budgeting means figuring out how much you can realistically afford to spend in a given area and still have enough for your two tithes and all other necessities. Then it means staying under that amount no matter what. It means imposing restrictions on yourself and then making yourself obey them.

To make a budget really work and to save money in the process, you need to learn one very important final principle.

Plan Your Spending in Advance

The most sure way in the world to let the various hucksters of the world—all very respectable, sincere, and reasonable appearing—swallow up our resources is to spend money without careful thought and planning. Buying impulsively almost never pays off in the long run. Nearly anything that is a legitimate and necessary expenditure can be predicted in advance. And you will wind up spending less by planning out these expenditures rather than taking them as they happen to come.

The two greatest monthly expenditures are usually rent or house payment and food. There is little that can be done to alter rent, but it is amazing how drastically you can cut your food bill by planning your trip to the market and adhering to the basic buying principles once you are there. Included in planning your marketing trips is planning menus in advance and then constructing a shopping list for those certain meals. You will find yourself much more organized as you go shopping and you will be less apt to linger in front of tempting items not on your list (at the pastry counter, for instance). You'll notice that as you buy only what you need, it is easier to adhere to sound eating principles, and that meal preparation itself is less time consuming and more enjoyable. You'll need to spend less time shopping and fixing meals. And all with the happy result of spending less money too!

And as you shop, remember the other principles—compare prices; look for bargains (from your list only!); buy slowly, not rashly; check ingredients; and stay away from expensive luxury foods. Study the principles in Chapter One of Part II on wise eating; think them through in light of financial wisdom, and learn to work your conclusions into your shopping patterns. You will be amazed at the results of your diligence.

My wife, Judy, has studied her shopping patterns, comparing totals with or without planned weekly menus. She has found that planning alone can save up to $30 a month simply from the wise buying it produces. It drastically cuts down on impromptu buying which for me, at least, is more devastating at a grocery store than anywhere. When you consider that a $20-$30 savings monthly would add up to close to $1500 in a five-year period, the reasons for wise food buying become economically significant as well.

These few principles—buying necessities, eliminating impulse buying, tearing up the credit cards, careful comparing, curbing appetites, setting limits for yourself, and planning—can help you cut your spending down to rock bottom when you are facing extreme circumstances. There will also be times which can be approached with more flexibility. These principles will always apply, but the specifics will vary in individual situations.

For instance, in our bookstore business we buy almost exclusively on credit. It is nearly impossible to manage a large enterprise otherwise. My wife and I, however, don't make personal purchases "on time." There have been times I have made spur of the moment purchases as well. It is something I try to avoid, but with time and experience I have found that I am gradually learning to distinguish good buys from poor ones. You will find the same thing. As you do, you will be able to adapt them to your own particular needs with wider limits. You must never relax your dedication to eliminate waste and foolish buying. But as God blesses you above your bare necessities, you can begin to analyze your priorities with a little more latitude— assuming you are faithfully saving your two tithes and adhering to the other principles. Flexibility does not mean you can start charging because now you can afford it. No, but you can begin to count nickels and dimes rather than pennies.

When You Must, You Can Save Large Amounts

A couple we know came to us three years ago in deep financial trouble. They were $6500 in debt and he was out of work. They were at the end of their rope.

It was the classic case of financial mismanagement. They owed BankAmericard (with interest), Sears (with interest), Wards (with interest), drugstores, gas stations, and a finance company (with *high* interest). They had bought on time, and foolishly. They had nothing to show for all their spending—no home, no quality furniture or new appliances. Their car (not an expensive one, quite old) had just been repossessed. I have no idea where their money had gone. It seemed to have been literally "poured through a sieve."

In spite of few visible assets, the bills nevertheless were there every month. They owed $200 a month in interest charges alone.

They came to us and said, "We need help. Would you take over our money, put us on a budget, and see if you can help us get out of debt?"

We sat down together and planned out a strategy. They recognized their need to be tightly controlled and their own inability to crack down on themselves. So we opened a joint bank account and I very tightfistedly began doling out their money.

We set up a poverty-level budget: cancelled the newspaper (only $3 a month), destroyed all the credit cards, cancelled all other charge accounts, and began to operate from a weekly allowance which at first included only $1 spending money. I doled out wash money in 10¢ and 25¢ increments and put every extra dime towards the bills.

I was a miser with their money.

We spent the next year and a half on this budget, part of which time he was on unemployment. When he *was* working he put in for overtime at every opportunity. And God blessed their honest efforts to get their spending habits back on the right track. As amazing as it might seem, they managed to live on less than $300 some months (and this was right in the midst of the energy inflation crisis which hit us so hard in the early 1970s). This was extremely hard on them. (It would have been for anyone. I'm not sure I would have been able to accomplish what they did.) Tensions occasionally arose over decisions we had to make. They were living on a poverty level and it hurt.

My point is this: amazing things are possible if one makes a commitment and sticks to it. After several months of irregular employment, his mill job became steady once again and the bills began to decrease. In a year and a half they were gone—$6500 in just eighteen months!

Consider that in this space of time his salary and unemployment benefits had totalled about $16,000; he saved and put toward his bills a whopping 40% of his income—before taxes and before his church giving (which we began at 2% and increased by 1/2% per month). For a family on a very modest mill salary, that is quite an accomplishment.

When urgent necessity demands it, we can use our money much more wisely than we ordinarily do.

One final comment: Trust the Lord with your money. This is not said lightly, a tacked on catch-all phrase. It is foundational. For two reasons you should take your finances to prayer often: so you can keep money in its proper balance in your life, and so that God can use and bless the money He has given you. If you have a financial need, God knows about it. Leave it in His hands. He is able to perform miracles with money. He can multiply it or bring it in from unexpected sources. Don't depend on your own clever means. Stick to the principles we have discussed and allow God to provide.

The Flow

Once you have a fairly tight control on your finances you will begin to see your money used and multiplied in ever greater ways. As a tool, money can be used rightly or wrongly. A wrench can cause a leak or fix one. A gun can save a life or take one. All tools must be used knowledgeably and wisely to do their best work. Money, therefore, must always be kept in perspective. God wants His people to prosper so He can make use of this tool. But in order to do so, He must make sure His people are money-wise so that the tool will be wielded effectively.

God desires that we prosper for two reasons. One, simply for our own happiness and well-being. God wants to bless His people; He delights in blessing His people. He wants to lavishly provide all our needs. Of course, many times His deepest blessings come to us through adversity. But ordinarily adversity is a temporary thing. Though God allowed Job to be stripped of everything, He blessed the end of Job's life with much greater wealth than He had at the beginning (Job 42:12). But God simply cannot shower all manner of prosperity on us because we wouldn't know how to use it wisely. So He must do it slowly, mixing in adversity and want so we learn to trust Him for everything, teaching us wisdom along the way.

Secondly, God desires that we prosper to increase our capacity for giving. The more resources at our disposal and submitted to the carrying out of God's instructions, the greater will be God's opportunities to minister to the needs of people through us. Particularly as conditions in the world grow more difficult for a majority of people (which is happening already), God wants us to have the means to provide food, clothing, shelter, Bibles, and so on, for those in need of them. For money does allow such service to happen.

This is not to say that ministering to others is totally dependent on money. Not at all. Primarily God wants a people whose hearts are submitted to Him and are therefore being transformed into the image of Jesus. This submission and utter reliance on God is the foundation for all significant love and service. God expects us to behave as Jesus did in all areas of our lives.

Once that moment-by-moment trusting relationship with God does exist, He is able to increase the impact we can have for the good of those around us. Therefore, once we come to a willingness to let God use us in any way He chooses, He will usually increase our supply so that we might in turn increase our giving.

There are two rudimentary precepts of spiritual prosperity in operation here. The first is: God is the source of prosperity—the *only* source. Without God's blessing we will not succeed. People do get rich without God. But such people have money, *not* prosperity. Prosperity refers to one's total condition of life—physical, spiritual, social, mental. It is something only God can provide. Abundant goods are only one aspect of prosperity. When God prospers, He brings physical well-being, peace, wisdom, spiritual insight, servanthood, and the other fruits of the spirit as well. It was this total prosperity God gave to Solomon (for a time). Read the book of Proverbs for numerous (hundreds!) of examples of how prosperity, wisdom and trust in the Lord are woven tightly together.

The second principle of prosperity is this: it comes from giving. God will not prosper you or me for our sakes' alone. He gives so that we in turn may give. He uses us and what He gives us to bless others. We are channels through which His abundance can flow.

The world views wealth as something we accumulate—better things, larger net worth, more cash in the bank, and so on. But in God's economy wealth is measured by how much flows out from us rather than how much we retain. The difference between the two may be seen by comparing a water tank and a water pipe. The tank holds so many gallons, say 100,000. The pipe, on the other hands, *holds* very little water, maybe a few gallons. But it has the capacity to deliver many times 100,000 gallons that are pumped through. Water in the tank just sits; water in the pipe is always flowing. God wants to abundantly prosper you so you will be able to give. He wants to get the flow going, from

Him, through you, and out to others. That is true prosperity.

Picture it another way. The water pipes in your home are full of water. They are connected to the boundless city supply and the water is ready at any moment to flow into your house. Millions of gallons are there for your use, only a few feet away.

But not a single drop will actually flow into your home until you turn on a faucet and let it flow out. The moment you do, however, you are tapped into a supply that is endless. As long as you leave that line open water will flow out uninterrupted. There will never be a shortage because every gallon of water that flows out is replaced by a gallon flowing in from the city reservoir. Exactly what flows out flows in from the other end.

But the moment you shut off the outward flow by turning off the faucet, the in-flow stops as well. They cease simultaneously.

God's provision is like that. We are tapped in to an infinite source of supply of every kind—wealth, peace, joy, freedom, health, and wisdom. And the only prerequisite for the abundance from that source flowing into and over every facet of our lives is that we turn on the outflow faucet and allow God's goodness to flow from us to those about us. As we do, God's blessings flow into us. The greater the outward flow from us, the greater the incoming flow will be from God. It will flow from God to us in ever-increasing amounts as long as it is flowing right through us and out again. God's supply diminishes accordingly as we turn off the flow to others. Like the water pipes, it is just impossible for more to flow in than flows out. You cannot store it up. There is no "holding tank" for the blessings and prosperity of God.

The analogy breaks down at a very crucial point, however. For in God's system, the more you give, the larger your capacity to give will become. Your pipes will actually increase in size the faster the water moves through them. As long as you allow the process to continue, the flow will keep increasing and increasing.

The point isn't that God expects you to give away everything He gives you. There are many aspects to the prosperity He desires for you, one of which is simply to bless you because He loves you. He does expect, however, that you make wise and prudent use of it all, always prayerfully considering every opportunity you have to give. Everyone will not be led of God to give in precisely the same manner either. God distributes many talents, only some of which are financial. But whatever God has given you, the key to its full blessing is the realization that you cannot grasp and hold onto it. As George MacDonald once said, "In heaven the books you will truly own and derive the greatest pleasure from are those dog-eared old copies you lent out many times or gave away, not the ones that remained neatly on your shelf."

PART V

PREPARING OUR FAMILIES FOR THE FUTURE

As I jog around our neighborhood in the early morning hours before most households are yet astir, I cannot help but wonder, "Everything seems so tranquil; could all this gloomy preoccupation with the future be nothing but hollow fears? Won't mankind's existence simply continue on as it has for years . . . ?"

Though I am aware that "all have sinned, and come short of the glory of God," on the whole it seems that most people aren't so wicked that if turned loose they would instantly throw bombs, burn houses, kill, plunder, and try to destroy everything around them. "Most people are ordinary enough," I think to myself. "Won't this great 'normality' of the masses somehow stabilize things in the world?"

With further consideration, however, I have to admit that if I'd been jogging in my neighborhood in 1929, I could well have been thinking the same things. Or if I'd been walking streets in England or France in 1937, everything would have appeared peaceful and "normal" enough, but I'd have been greviously wrong.

Doom and crisis and death and destruction and poverty were so close you could have smelled them if your senses had been keen enough. Depression and war were right around the corner. And they were destined to effect everyone.

No, world events are not usually directed by the average, ordinary person living in a tranquil neighborhood. Even though such people may comprise an immense majority, they get swept up in circumstances bigger than they are. Events that change the course of world history have never had a high regard for the composed and undisturbed lives of ordinary citizens.

Once the peaceful homes awake and bustle with life and activity as the day proceeds, I see growing evidence all around, however subtle, of Satan's determination to wrestle control of the world from the hand of God. We may not always recognize it, but a war is going on!

Therefore I must continually remind myself that the relative harmony I feel when playing on the lawn with my children is not a true measure of the state of the world. If it were 1939 and we were playing in an English village five miles from the English Channel, it would be hard to forget. The distant ominous rumble of machinery and roar of planes and guns would serve as continual reminder that things were happening in the world beyond my limited sights—things that could one day infringe upon the peace of my family and could well destroy my home and front lawn altogether. My heart would pound in constant readiness to sweep my sons in my arms and whisk them away to protection from what might suddenly break out close at hand.

But today we play on the lawn and no war planes are in the sky, no frightening sounds of tanks and mortar shells come from just beyond our sight. Instead we look up and point excitedly to the Goodyear Blimp, in town for a special promotion, lit with bright colors and a "happy face" and huge letters for all to see: "Have a nice day!"

It is easy to get lulled to sleep.

But these are different times than they seem. A new day is on the horizon—a day that may mean persecution and deprivation more severe than any people have yet experienced it. Satan's attack will be total and unrelenting and God's people will bear the brunt of much of it.

So when I hear someone say, "Isn't it exciting to be living in the last days?" I often wonder to myself if "exciting" is quite the proper word. God has no doubt blessed us immeasurably in choosing us to be part of these times. But realizing I could be called upon to give my life because of my faith arouses many, many emotions inside me.

When I am playing on the lawn with my boys, therefore, and we all point up to the blimp together and laugh and talk about it, inside I have to ask as well, "How can I prepare these boys for the things they may someday face?"

The thought that they may be martyred as God's servants before they reach my age is very sobering. "These are the sons God has given me," I think. "He has given them to me for a short time to prepare them for their future. They could be part of God's army that will one day face the might of Satan himself. An ordinary faith in God will do them little good when that time comes. God has called them to live and serve in unique times."

They are called to be mighty men of God. As anything less, they cannot survive.

God has given me the gigantic responsibility of molding these little mounds of clay, according to His purpose, into vessels which will be called upon to pour out His life like no people before.

1

Preparing the Next Generation for God

Courage, Leadership, Wisdom, and Compassion

What can I build into my children to enable them to face the coming days fully as God's children? If I could open them up and deposit into their hearts and minds and spirits certain qualities, what would they be? If I could mold their lives as perfectly as a skilled sculpter fashions a pliable lump of clay, what characteristics would I choose to give them? What would the finished product look like?

In my idealism many attributes quickly spring to mind: faith in God, confidence, love, security, peace, tenderness, stamina, knowledge, self-control, trust, submissiveness, understanding, joy, patience, fruitfulness, kindness, perseverence, modesty, gentleness, obedience, sensitivity, worshipfulness, open-mindedness, goodness, praising heart, humility, serving spirit, calmness, cheerfulness, and thankfulness.

Of course what father, especially a Christian father, wouldn't give his son or daughter such characteristics if there was any way he could do so? But can one even hope to begin such a task? Has the person yet lived who has exhibited all of these traits?

Only one. And Luke says of Jesus that He *increased* in wisdom and in stature and in favor with God and man (Luke 2:52), which implies that His wisdom and favor grew from something less to something more. Because of His surroundings, His experiences, His attitudes, His learning, and—probably most important of all—the training of His father and mother, Jesus *increased* in wisdom and other godly characteristics.

That gives me great inspiration, knowing that Jesus was taught and molded in such a way that His wisdom increased as He grew. It must, therefore, be possible for me also to contribute to the nurturing and flowering of these characteristics in my own children. Of course I cannot control and predict every detail of my child's life. But I must behave as if such were indeed possible and then, as Mary and Joseph must have done, leave the final result in the hands of God.

In these critical days, therefore, I see as probably my single highest priority the significant preparation of my family, especially my children, for the years ahead. They are presently in my hands to shape and influence and make ready for perilous times. And the most beneficial provision I can make for their future is to instill within them the qualities of courage, leadership, wisdom, and compassion.

If my example is to have one result in the lives of my children, I pray daily it is this: that all I am as a person (my character, growth, spiritual maturity, sensitivity, wisdom, leadership, and love) will combine with the training and teaching I give them to produce lifelong courage, leadership, wisdom, and compassion within them.

As God unfolds the answer to this prayer over the years, my family will gradually develop the Christlikeness necessary to face the unknown future with head high, knowing God to be both on the throne and by their side. Maybe it is for myself I pray. Maybe it is I who realize I lack the courage to face what may be across the channel, over the sea, beyond tomorrow—the unknown. Maybe my most serious preparation should be for myself. For only God knows what my family and I might have to face together. In a moment of trial, their husband and father will be looked to for courage and wisdom and leadership. The effectiveness of my preparation, for us all, will be on the line. I hope they can look into my face in that moment and see a reflection of God. And I hope I will look into their faces and see a reflection of angels singing.

I have rarely been so sobered as when I read the following account. I think it hit me so hard because I realized the day could come when God would require such courage of me and of my own sons and wife. Whether it be on the high seas, in a cold dark prison, in a furious storm, in a bloody war, or as Satan unleashes the wrath of his servants upon us, it is for such a day I am preparing my family.

When George Jaeger took his three sons and his elderly father out on the Atlantic Ocean for a fishing trip, he had no premonition of the horror that he would face in a matter of hours. Before he would step on shore again, Jaeger would watch each son and then his father die, victims of exhaustion and lungs filled with water.

The boat's engine had stalled in the late afternoon. While increasing winds had whipped the sea into great waves, the boat rolled helpless in the water and then began to list dangerously. When it became apparent that they were sinking, the five Jaeger men put on the life vests, tied themselves together with a rope, and slipped into the water. It was 6:30 P.M. when the sinking craft disappeared and the swimmers set out to work their way toward shore.

Six-foot waves and a strong current made the swimming almost impossible. First one boy, and then another—and another . . . swallowed too much water. Helpless, George Jaeger watched his sons and then his father die. Eight hours later, he staggered onto the shore, still pulling the rope that bound the bodies of the other four to him.

"I realized they were all dead—my three boys and my father—but I guess I didn't want to accept it, so I kept swimming all night long," he told reporters. "My youngest boy, Clifford, was the first to go. *I had always taught our children not to fear death* because it was being with Jesus Christ. Before he died I heard him say, 'I'd rather be with Jesus than go on fighting.' "

Performance under stress is one test of effective leadership. It may also be the proof of accomplishment when it comes to evaluating the quality of a father. In that awful Atlantic night, George Jaeger had a chance to see his three sons summon every ounce of courage and self-control he had tried to build into them. The beautiful way they died said something about the kind of father George Jaeger had been for fifteen years.

Few fathers will have their leadership-effectiveness tested so dramatically or so suddenly. For most men, the test will come in small doses over a long period of living. But the test comes to all, and sooner or later the judgment is rendered. . . . All five people in that dangerous situation required every bit of strength derived from the relationships they had forged over the years.[21]

No, the Lord may not so dramatically test the effectiveness of my leadership and accomplishment in the lives of my boys. But in the uncertain times ahead there is no assurance that He won't find such a thing necessary either. "The test comes to all, and sooner or later the judgment is rendered."

"Lord," I sigh, "I couldn't face what he did. I love them too much."

"But I love them too," He answers, "even more than you do. And remember, I lost a son myself. I gave Him up for a higher good, a greater love. I may call upon you to do the same thing. Because I love you and I love your sons. The days ahead will require sacrifice and giving. You may be chosen to partake of the same cup of sorrow that I had to drink in losing my only son. If you are so chosen, drink the cup with courage, as George Jaeger did."

Realizing that one day my sons and my wife and I could be standing side-by-side before a firing squad because we all professed Jesus to be our Lord is not a thought to dismiss lightly. In that moment I want to be able to say, "I had always taught my children. . . ." Even if my youngest were only ten, in that moment God would call upon him to be a man.

The growth and nurturing of that manhood is presently in my hands.

Elements Necessary to Nurture the Character of Your Child

What then are the things I can do now while my children are young that will bring to flower these qualities of Jesus in later years? How can I help to make them into the sort of persons who will be able to face the unknown with a deep trust in God? Though to do so would be convenient, it is not possible to deposit qualities into them the same way we feed information to our brain to prepare it for an exam. Spiritual qualities are internal. They must originate from within a person's heart. All we can do for our children is to provide soil, water and care to make the conditions most favorable for that growth to take place. God is the one who breathes life and spiritual health into each one. There are, however, several things we can do to see that the soil and conditions for growth are optimum. Being aware daily of these ingredients for healthy growth will insure that the best conditions exist for God to be able to bring our children to their maximum potential.

Have a Plan

We must have a goal clearly established in our minds as to what kind of person we want our child to be and what we can do to reach that goal. Most parents embark on the raising of their children with no detailed plan of action. They have not visualized the end result, nor have they thought through a plan for accomplishing their goals. They simply take each day, each new event and each new development in their child's life as it chances to come. Children grow at random when such a procedure is followed.

Christian parents have a high responsibility to do otherwise. We must think through where we are trying to go as parents. However it comes—from books, from teaching, from counseling, from talking with others, from observing other parents and children, from our study of the Bible, from our talks as husband and wife—we must arrive at a plan for the spiritual character growth of our children. God will call them to be mighty men and women. We cannot take lightly our charge as their parents and merely "hope" they grow up to "serve the Lord." Accidents do not happen here. At present our children are but unformed clay. God has given them to us for a time to create the conditions in which He can mold them into men and women who are prepared for all that will be required of them.

Within every child is vast potential lying dormant, waiting to be brought to the surface. They are placed under our authority and care to either reach that potential or else fall short of it. To see that they do is one of the most important tasks of our lives, though often that truth is not realized until it is much too late. Fragmentary efforts, some effective and good, some harmful, but with no plan encompassing the whole leads both parents and children into the future without an adequate base to face the demands upon them.

Establishment of Parental Priorities

Parents often do not grasp the enormity of this truth that in many respects their child's future rests in their hands. What parents build into the growth and development of their child will largely determine many of the characteristics he will grow up to manifest. For the parent who would effectively nurture and train his child, the first step must be to determine where children fit into his life. Many become parents without having thought through the implications, without having given any significant consideration to what they hope to accomplish through parenthood.

For many parents, including many Christians, children are a side benefit to complement one's life, job, ministry, marriage, and the achievement of other goals. When this is the case there is not the intensity of vision poured into the child's everyday life. A parent's thoughts center about the immediate rather than the long-range nature of their molding influence over him. A child grows and matures, therefore, without a careful plan guiding the process.

Although this is often the way parenting is carried out, it is not effective, nor is it proper in light of the Scriptures. A glance through Proverbs or a look at Moses' commands to Israelite parents will show that God intended parenthood to be a well-thought-out, preoccupying way of life (Deut. 4:10; Deut. 6:7; Prov. 2:6-11; Prov. 23:12-13). This can never happen until parents have made the conscious decision that their children are their ultimate priority.

Training and Discipline

Once parents have set goals and established the priority of their children in their lives, the stage is set for them to begin the actual process of influencing their children. Visualize the raising of children similar to erecting a home; the foundation must be the disciplinary training you give him. There is something about discipline that is hard and firm, even unyielding, like the cement that undergirds a sturdy building. Discipline is a word sometimes considered ugly, often avoided, misused and abused. Nevertheless it is the foundation.

Many different aspects are inherent in effective training and therefore in a secure base. Far more than the word punishment (for which it is often mistaken), discipline implies authority, respect, obedience, love, consistency, parental responsibility, teaching and affection. Without *all* these factors at work, the foundation will not be all it should be. If you or I improperly discipline (for whatever reason and however done), we will build a weak and shaky support for the future lives of our children.

The problems with a weak foundation are obvious. The buildings in the Italian city of Venice are slowly sinking into the sea because they are built on wet, boggy ground—their foundations do not extend down to bedrock. The leaning tower in Pisa was built with an insufficient base as well. It could be saved only by digging down and refoundationing it with tons and tons of concrete. No matter how beautiful the building, the foundation determines its inherent strength and how long it will last.

There is a difference between buildings and children, however. Once the initial concrete is set in the life of a child, there is no going back to replace it.

Instilling Self-esteem

The nurturing of self-value is the most important task a parent faces—how a child feels about himself, his self-worth, his own appraisal of how his parents and God and other people view him. A child with a healthy dose of esteem regards himself highly and therefore has confidence and peace. Low esteem fills a child with feelings of inadequacy, worthlessness, and inferiority. He is sure that others do not like him because he does not like himself. Without supplying a child a proper regard for his own personhood, everything else a parent does, no matter how good, is in vain. Every day we stamp into our children attitudes, words, ideas, beliefs, habits, and responses that will one day, when they are older and the shape of the clay has been set, be an automatic part of them. What we say and how we react can either build or destroy. The impressions we create in their early years set the stage for an entire trend in life. Our responses to their first attempts at independence, at personhood in their own right, will shape their personalities, motivations, dreams, abilities, and views. Everything we say and do has a tremendous inner effect on the shaping and molding process taking place—*everything*!

Without a high self-esteem built into his child, no parent can even hope to inculcate into that child's personality and heart even a fraction of the qualities mentioned earlier. For high self-esteem is at the very core of how we relate to God. We can never fully accept and experience God's magnificent love and provision if we are crippled by a feeling of inadequacy, because it will be nearly impossible for us to fully grasp that He completely loves us regardless of anything. A parent's enormous responsibility to make his child feel accepted and valuable is at the heart of that child's entire relationship to God.

This huge and necessary aspect of parenthood is accomplished by giving your child a healthy and positive feeling about himself daily through approval of what he does, affirmation of who he is, appreciation, encouragement, and praise.

Teaching Your Child

Like man-made computers, the brain of a child must be programmed to be used. If a child is given enough of the right input throughout his first few years of life, his brain can be programmed for learning and absorbing all that life has to offer. His horizons can be stretched for the rest of his life.

God has placed within every human being an instinctive hunger to learn. From the moment of birth babies, then toddlers, then schoolchildren, chase after knowledge furiously. It is a basic drive. Nothing you do or refuse to do will keep this from happening. And with help and guidance and healthy motivation, they will even learn faster, will enjoy it more, will keep learning longer, and will learn truth.

Visualize the universe designed as a classroom, and the home a microcosm of it. For the young child the home *is* the universe, and his parents are the teachers. A child can drift through life learning and absorbing whatever chances to come his way. Or he can be guided through life by parents who provide the stimulus which allow him to mature and learn rapidly in a godly direction.

The teaching a parent provides his child determines the size of his world. The more diverse the teaching patterns, the more abundant a child's life will be, the larger will be the home which his spirit will occupy, and the wider will be the range and depth of his character as he faces the future.

The most significant teaching a parent provides springs from a child's curiosity. The wise parent nurtures this as the child grows in imagination and creativity. Intelligence, interest in life, creativity, and excitement all have their roots in the imagination. A mind that probes the unusual, the new, the curious, the unknown is a mind more able to know itself and probe the hidden reaches of God's world, His principles, and His infinite character.

Parents can enrich their children in these creative areas by their own attitude toward life. And there are two kinds of experiences children should have often. First, outside influences of infinite variety—from the zoo to a camping trip to making a dress with Mom or helping Dad with a project in the shop—every experience is a learning one for a child. Secondly, children need quality time with each parent when life is given perspective not only through shared activities but also through discussion. As a child grows such times provide the basis for talking about God's principles and about the future. But the impact of discussion is proportionate to the times that have been spent sharing activities. Parent's accomplish very little using the classroom method—sitting down for periodic "lessons." For children are learning from their parents every moment. Everything we are—both toward them and to others, our attitudes and responses and character—provides the foundation for our direct verbal interaction. Through our words, we teach our children in two ways. We are passing along information to them about life and the world, information which they need in greater amounts as they mature. We are also instilling attitudes, responses, values, and priorities; not simply by what we tell them *about* God and life and our responsibility toward others, but also by how adequately we live up to our own words. The brain of a child works overtime, taking raw information and words, and assimilating it, organizing it, analyzing it, and forming life-molding attitudes and patterns deep in the subconscious. Our children carefully observe not only *what* we say, but also *how* we say it and *how* we live it. We are primarily models during their formative years when everything (both heard and observed) leaves an indelible impression. Habits, reflexes, values, and qualities of character are implanted by our own actions and responses as well as by words. Every moment of a relationship between a child and his father or mother is an essential part of this complex training and teaching process.

Implanting Spiritual Perspectives

Through our experiences with our children we must deliberately develop spiritual values and priorities. We cannot leave them to pick up accidentally a spiritual value structure and outlook on life; it must be inculcated over the years by us, their constant teachers. A growing child needs to be told about God—not from a doctrinal slant but from an intensely personal one. All spiritual training must come from this angle—that God is very intimately a part of the family. With this foundation, later personal introduction to Jesus will be very natural and real.

Telling our children about God and the Bible and the church, reading the Bible and praying with them, taking them to church are of course part of the training process. But as we've mentioned earlier, the most important part of our spiritual training must be the example of our own lives. In teaching them verbally about the Lord, about truth, obedience, prayer, respect, and faith, we must recognize that their most basic learning does not come with our telling. It comes later as they witness those principles coming to life before their eyes—in *our* lives. How do we live and react? What do they hear me say and see me do when the hammer slams down on my thumb, when the traffic is snarled, or when the roof and hot water heater begin to leak at the same time?

Being a parent means I am on the job day and night, filling my children with perspectives on life by my own life. If they grow to see my actions line up with those things I have *told* them about God's principles, then they will sense order and will accept what I tell them as reasonable. They will be secure in that consistency and will be all the more likely to later accept our system of spiritual values as their own.

Providing a Model of Leadership

The model a parent provides his children has two components. First he (with all his values, convictions, attitudes, and actions) is constantly on display before his children. This provides substance to their present life as well as future memories. If a parent is consistent it will provide a great security, a covering to keep erosion of secularism from undermining the values he has instilled into the life of his child.

The parental model, however, is not a static thing. You are a daily pattern to your children, not only by the things you stand for but by the things you do. Beyond merely a model, you are also their leader. You provide a solidarity to their lives by what you are; you lead them and show them life by what you do.

Both of these perspectives on a parent's role are vital.

In one sense this is to a greater degree a father's function than a mother's. Though of course a wife complements her husband's role, it is uniquely the father whom God has called to be the leader in family relationships. His task is to institute order and then to maintain it, to guide children through the years into maturity so that they can experience and blossom into the full potential God intended for them.

God has given to the man in the family this unusual opportunity. And it is a responsibility for which he will be held accountable. If a child is not allowed to thrive to the very reaches of his potential, it is first of all to the father one must look for the reason. The mother contributes significantly. Yet the father provides the foundational drive and momentum to see the job through to the end.

The father is a leader from whom two things are constantly required—one positive, one negative. On the negative side, he is the one who must lay a firm foundation of authority in his child's life in order to stay the rebellion which can develop in his heart. But on the positive side, once this foundation is laid a father is called upon to guide his family on a daily exploration of everything in life God has placed here for us to discover. In that process of discovery, both the father and mother become daily models. All of a child's earliest reactions to life, experiences, and relationships with other people are tightly bound up in the reactions they observe in their parents. All human experience is reflected through parents to their children. This process continues day and night, whether or not any of the participants is the least bit aware of it. When a child begins to develop habits, values, and patterns of response of his own, he will largely mirror the early demonstrations of leadership exhibited by his parents.

Preparing a Child for the Future

A parent does *not* prepare his son or daughter for things he may someday face by *telling* him what those things may be. The parent who would genuinely prepare his son or daughter for the future must provide a framework in his life from which God can form him into a certain type of person. A person is not prepared because he possesses information; he is prepared by virtue of who and what he *is*. Parents, therefore, equip their children by giving them capabilities, attitudes, habits, and values which, when the times of testing come, see them through as mature sons and daughters of God.

In the trying days that are coming upon the world, parents now have the responsibility of adequately preparing the next generation, their children, as effectively as they can for the things they may face. Parents must seize upon every opportunity to instill responsibility, courage, and maturity into their children without pressuring them to grow up faster than they are able. Children need to learn to make decisions through years of practice, beginning with small issues. Children are also prepared by being taught skills and capabilities and how to use them.

If the foundational and structural elements in the life of a child have been squarely built, it will be a joy to parents to watch this process of gradually increasing maturity and independence unfold. As a child learns to accept himself as capable through his increasing responsibility and through our unconditional acceptance, he will learn to step out positively all the more. His increasing independence (in an entirely positive, not rebellious, sense,) will be rooted in his assurance of his parents' dependability and his own personhood before God.

Parents also prepare their children for the future by building into their lives from a very early age the capacity to deal with different kinds of stresses. If our approach to doubts and problems (by example as well as teaching) is calm and deliberate and is based on a deep trust in God, such patterns will find their way into a child's habit patterns.

There is a certain rigorous conditioning which must be infused over the years—the tough self-discipline to withstand and weather adversities. This is a personal quality that is inbred into a child largely from observing his parents. But we can train our children to deal with challenges they will face as well, through the planned or unplanned stresses we carefully and gently allow to tug on their emotional equilibrium.

Through such conditioning we teach our children that surface feelings can be mastered and conquered, that barriers can be broken down, and, above all, that God can always be completely trusted in every circumstance.

Don't Stop Here—Keep Reading!

This chapter has been quite different from most that have preceded it. In each section up till now it has been my intention to provide you with concrete things you can do to prepare for the future. As I ambitiously embarked on the subject of preparing your families for the future, however, I realized there was really no way to adequately provide down-to-earth, helpful suggestions short of writing another entire book. For what is parenthood but preparing one's children for their future? I am aware that the whole scope of parenthood is involved in the title of the chapter itself.

What I have decided to do, therefore, is simply establish the need for parents to equip their families for the coming years and then to direct them to other sources for more specific instructions on how they can accomplish that.

I want to make clear that this chapter has been but an introduction to this whole subject. You definitely do need to go elsewhere for the specific, daily advice on how to do the things we have discussed. Because of the importance of this subject, I stress the necessity of further reading.

My own book, for instance, *Blueprint for Raising a Child,* deals in depth with these things we just touched upon—disciplinary training, instilling self-esteem, spiritual perspectives, and so on. And there are many other excellent ones you should be using as well: *Dare to Discipline, Hide or Seek, The Christian Family, The Effective Father,* and others listed in the appendices. I encourage you to consult these other sources.

PART VI
PREPARING FOR THE FUTURE SPIRITUALLY

Although what follows comes toward the end, in many ways it is foundational for everything else we have discussed. Without these preparatory spiritual principles operating in your life, whatever other measures you seek to follow will not accomplish their complete work.

Much of life is based on attitude. Often what might have been perfectly good action or word is nullified by a sour attitude. Similarly, the principles of preparation in this book are dependent on spiritual perspective to bring them to life. You may carry them out rigorously, but without the proper spiritual attitude toward what you are doing, they will prove valueless.

Three men working side-by-side on a bricklaying project were asked about the nature of their work. The first said, "I am laying bricks"; the second, "I am building a wall." But the third man, doing precisely the same thing as the others, responded, "I am raising a great cathedral."

Several years ago I was stopped short when I read in *Hind's Feet on High Places*, "The Lord is not doing so much *through* us as He is *in* us."

I was at the time heavily involved in all sorts of Christian activities and projects in our church. I thought the Lord was accomplishing some good "through" me. I couldn't get this statement out of my mind. It forced me to stop to evaluate God's primary purpose in my life.

What began to unfold to me was something quite different than I had previously imagined. I had assumed that God was primarily in the business of "saving the world" and that we were His agents to help with the process. But now I began to realize that such was not God's number-one purpose at all. What God wants even more than a saved world is a *people of a particular type.* He wants a people set apart, a people holy and pure, a transformed people—a people who are like Jesus (1 Pet. 2:9-10).

Such a people will be seen as individuals and as a body, a unit. Separately they will demonstrate very unique personal characteristics of behavior (Matt. 5, 6, 7; Gal. 5:22-23). And corporately they will exhibit a unity that transcends every aspect of life.

When this truth began opening up to me, I realized that God's principle aim in my life had to be something internal rather than what He was accomplishing externally through me. He intended to transform me into someone who behaved uniquely as an individual and who displayed an unusual sort of relationship with other Christians.

Accepting this, as I looked ahead to the future I saw this personal and corporate transformation as crucial. I saw that I had to allow God to make me personally into someone more like Jesus, and had to allow Him to make me part of a Church which is being made into a perfected bride for Jesus when He returns.

If I tried to prepare myself for the future apart from God's larger plan of transforming me and preparing His Church, my preparedness would be incomplete.

1

Unity and Community

End Times Unity

Most Christians agree one scriptural sign of the last days will be a remarkable unity between God's people on earth. Jesus prayed (John 17:11) that His followers might all be "one" and Paul taught (Eph. 5:27) that the Church will one day be presented to Christ "holy and without blemish." And many look with excitement at current signs which seem to indicate this oneness is indeed already beginning to manifest itself. The "Jesus explosion" of young people in recent years has been almost void of denominational lines; in the main line Protestant churches there is a noticeable loosening of denominational ties; the Charismatic movement has made great strides toward overcoming once-inflexible restrictions and has superseded denominational boundaries, involving Christians from all parts of the spectrum from Catholics to Pentecostals; there is a visible feeling of acceptance and goodwill between Catholics and Protestants which was nonexistent fifteen years ago.

The assumption from all this has been that if end-times unity has not arrived, at least it is well on its way.

These manifestations we are seeing are good things, indications of a thriving and healthy Church. Yet as I observe them, I wonder if it is going to require a deeper look to find the true sort of unity God intends us to have one day. For though these directions are all good, what we are witnessing is unity based primarily on organization and doctrine. It is easy to assume we are "one" with a person because we have some rather significant things in common. Charismatics have long made this serious error, as have other groups who have shared backgrounds and experiences. In a large Charismatic meeting, for instance, where most everyone knows the same songs, worships in a similar manner, speaks in tongues, lifts hands in praise, and prays in the Spirit, the conclusion is drawn that everyone is "one." Where many people of various persuasions share a common purpose or vision and see the need to carry it out in a similar manner, it is assumed that everyone present is "one in Christ" because agreement has come out of such a diverse gathering of people.

There is a unity present, to be sure. But it is organizational and doctrinal. A ladies' auxiliary or men's lodge gathering could boast the same kind of unity. It is a perfectly good thing, but there is nothing uniquely Christian about it.

It is clear the sort of harmony that God's people will one day demonstrate will be much deeper. It will be a distinctive sort of bond between hearts and lives—a bond that will carry over into every conceivable area of existence. It will be a bond that will prepare us to meet Jesus as His perfected bride.

Not Sameness but a Relationship in the Midst of Differences

I am not for a moment suggesting that I am capable of giving you a simple definition of true biblical unity. In fact, it is so deep and foreign to our limited imaginations that we cannot hope to comprehend it in finite terms. But I do have an idea of some of its results. Like the scientist who understands the atom, not by observing it but by watching the effects it has on its surroundings, maybe we can get at a working understanding of unity by looking at some of the results.

Have you ever discovered yourself in a situation where you and one other shared something unique? Possibly you walked into a certain class on the first day of the fall term to find there was only one other male (or female) in the class of thirty. Though you didn't know him or may have been completely unlike him, you would have an immediate bond with that other man.

When I was in Germany, the moment I heard a bit of English in a crowd, my ears perked up. I knew there was something deep and personal I shared with someone else close by. I may not have yet have even seen a face to associate with the voice, but I knew we shared something important—language.

Imagine yourself living in the deepest reaches of Norway in a village of five thousand people. You speak no Norwegian and none of the villagers speak English. Your culture probably will be entirely different from theirs as well. Then one day another English-speaking family moves in across town—an immediate bond. It will not be long before you will know one another well. You may have completely different backgrounds, different beliefs, different values, different moral standards, different religious convictions, and a different ethnic heritage. Yet the bond cementing you together among so many foreigners will vastly outweigh all those differences. You will undoubtedly become friends.

I have an idea the unity Christians will one day demonstrate to the world will be something like that. It will be a unity that exists in the face of huge and overwhelming surface differences.

There are hundreds of things that draw Christians together, but up till this point they usually have been rather superficial: shared beliefs, experiences, doctrines, attitudes, backgrounds, and common interests—even ethnic heritage. Churches themselves are gatherings of people who believe in certain similar things. Church creeds, covenants, and statements of faith articulate these doctrinal stances which churches take to differentiate themselves from other churches and groups. Liberals share and feel a bond because they have similar liberal views. Charismatics share and experience what they term unity because they have had similar experiences and share a common attitude toward the work of the Holy Spirit. Catholics feel a bond with other Catholics because of a tradition and background that is Catholic. Baptists, Lutherans, and Presbyterians are the same way. Such bonds are part of us all, and for the most part they enrich our lives.

But before Jesus returns I think we will see tradition-oriented Episcopalians, fundamental Baptists, liberal Methodists, and Charismatics all sharing deeply as a vital part of Christ's body! Unity won't be dependent on shared beliefs or experiences. It will exist right in the face of drastic differences.

Let's face it. We are still rather tightly caught up in doctrinal biases. We tend to suspect (however slightly) other Christians whose views and attitudes and beliefs and experiences do not parallel our own.

In saying that our unity will one day transcend these artificial barriers does not imply that all church members and "good people" and anyone however remotely connected with any church, past or present, is automatically a Christian since Christian unity is such an all-inclusive thing. No, God's body is made up of believers who have accepted Him, trusted Him—born-again people. God's body of believers is in one sense a very narrow group. It contains a "peculiar people, a holy nation" (1 Pet. 2:9). We are set apart.

Though this narrow quality exists, however, from the *outside*, it is yet a very vast and inclusive body on the *inside*. It contains people from all backgrounds, churches, doctrinal stances, experiences, nationalities, and races. Some are not church members at all. No one can erect his own standards for inclusion in the body without tampering with the original membership requirement.

Functioning as a Community

What will be some of the practical ways this spiritual unity will demonstrate itself? Jesus made it clear that it will be visible to the world. It will not be enough simply for this accord to exist between us. If the world is to know that we are Christians and that Jesus is the Son of God, then it must observe a love flowing between us. This is how the world is able to measure the validity of Jesus' claims, by our visible and active love for each other (John 13:35). And it will have to be a love that transcends the barriers presently separating us.

One of the significant ways love of Christians toward one another will begin to be apparent to the world will be through our functioning as a community of people set apart from the world. Community will become an active word, describing our total interaction together, not simply a proximity living arrangement. Christians will begin to function as a community irrespective of location and doctrine and church home and other differences.

For instance, to return for a moment to our Norwegian village. Let's imagine further that a third English-speaking family moves into the area. There is instantly a small community of three families. They will begin to function together, interact together, band together, help each other, share with each other, etc. Though they may all be totally different in many ways, they will be unified on the basis of what binds them together, functioning as a community within the village—similar to the many foreign communities that exist as pockets within our own country. People of a certain common heritage band together and function together as a community.

The unity and community the Christian church will someday exhibit will be deeper and more profound than anything that has yet existed in the world. But there will be qualities in it much like the spirit of community which still sees the Pennsylvania Amish gather for a barn raising for one of their number. A symbolic gesture of sharing and camaraderie, it provides a profound glimpse as to why that people have successfully remained nearly pure and separated decade after decade through many generations.

There will one day again be a common spirit of giving among Christians much like the early church demonstrated when Paul collected money around the Mediterranean for the distressed local assembly in Jerusalem.

Community caring, giving, sharing, interacting.

It will not have the limitations of so many of our organizations of the past. If a mission in Africa is under persecution, Baptist, Covenant and Pentecostal churches won't ask, "Is it a Baptist, Covenant, or Pentecostal mission?" They will simply gather clothes and food, collect money, and send them along with some people to help the mission, no matter whose mission it is.

If a church in town is building a new school and needs help bulldozing, laying carpet, lifting beams into place, laying bricks, landscaping, or hammering nails, they won't have to rely on their own church members alone. Christians will come pouring in from all over the city, from every conceivable church, to help however they can.

If a Christian owns a business, other Christians will feel a certain loyalty to support him. Our present indifference will be gone. We will sense a *need* to support him, knowing that he is supporting us as well in other ways. Christians will band together in every possible way.

If a certain church is experiencing some financial problems, its only help won't have to come from its own denominational headquarters. Churches from its area (all of them) will pitch in and support by sending money and personnel and whatever is needed.

Pastors will meet together to interact and pray and share burdens and ministries. There will be no lines drawn, no hidden prejudices. Gone will be our sole interest in our own things. Our attitudes will be much broader toward other facets of God's body. Pastors and churches and groups won't simply tolerate one another's existence. They will excitedly and actively support and encourage one another and participate in life together as totally as possible.

Somehow God will make it possible that we cease to be so oriented toward ourselves and *our own* organization, *our own* Sunday school literature, holding *our own* meetings, giving money to *our own* missions, supporting *our own* outreach programs, and evangelists making the rounds of churches in their *own* denomination. Our eyes will somehow become unglued from this fixation we presently have and will begin to see the larger scope of what God is doing.

Christians will truly be living and practicing the Christian life as Jesus taught it. We will be obeying the words, commands, instructions, and example of Jesus in all we do. We won't, therefore, be continually preoccupied with the question of who and what is right. Non-Christians and nominal Christians will have little interest in being a part of what is going on in the church—the total obedience, the faithful living of the principles of the Bible, the community living so completely demonstrated. Living God's principles will be our primary concern. We won't care whether so-and-so speaks in tongues, worships on Saturday or Sunday, uses the King James or Living Bible, goes to church to stand and shout or to sit quietly and be edified, or was sprinkled or immersed. We will only care that we love Him practically, visibly, and daily.

This will be the beginnings of true community.[22]

Readying Ourselves Now for That Community

As Jesus' coming draws closer and closer, this community of Christians will become more and more visible. The distinction between the world and God's people at present is often vague; it is possible to straddle the fence without being noticed. But this middle ground will become impossible in the days ahead. To be a Christian will require enormous commitment as well as a certain risk; it will not be possible to simply drift along. Christians will mean business.

To survive Christians will *have* to band together. Community living and interacting will not be an option. Christians will either live as a family, a body, a community or else will be forced to live in the world. Christians will not be able to go it alone in the days ahead.

So to make ready for that sort of living, we need to seek every opportunity to live that way now. Whenever and however we can we need to seek out a wider range of relationships among God's people. This means more openness toward those different (denominationally and doctrinally) than ourselves. It means looking for opportunities to serve our brothers by making our talents and skills and resources available. It means using Christian businesses and ministries and professionals whenever possible instead of non-Christians. It means especially trying to get outside the narrow confines of our own thinking patterns.

The vague and shadowy glimpses of unity and community we are beginning to observe around us, though incomplete, are nevertheless the first signs that God is at work creating the proper conditions for His later more significant work. To allow Him a free hand we must be obediently applying the principles now.

2

The Real and the Passing

Wood and Hay, or Gold and Silver?

Most people spend their lives concerned with things

they later discover to have been insignificant. The Christian, however, who has committed all that he is and has to God, has not squandered his efforts on meaningless activities but has been used by God in every detail to mold and mature and purify him for the life to come. He is ready to face death calmly. He knows that because of God's work throughout his life he is ready for it.

But this will not be automatic. Being a Christian is no guarantee that your life is not being swallowed up by passing and temporal concerns. The Bible very specifically warns that it is possible for a child of God to spend his life seeking after the wrong things, building with materials that are of no value.

> Let each man take care how he builds. If anyone builds on the foundation which is Jesus Christ, with any material, whether it be with gold, silver, and fine stones or with wood, hay, and straw, the work that each man has done will one day be brought to light. . . . The fire will test the worth of each man's work. If the work which any man has built survives he will receive a reward; if it burns he will have to bear the loss, though he will escape with his life. (1 Cor. 3:10-15, author's paraphrase)

Does "building on the foundation" mean studying your Bible regularly so that you possess great insight concerning spiritual matters? witnessing regularly so that many become Christians as a result? having a variety of memorable experiences which draw you "closer to the Lord"? reading and studying spiritual books and topics? growing into a position of great respect and leadership in the church? or being raised up as a mightily used Bible teacher, preacher, author, counselor, or evangelist?

Is building with "gold, silver, and fine stones" reserved for what we might call "super saints," those men and women whom God seems to use greatly in everything they do—expounding the word, leading God's flock, witnessing to the lost—and whose lives boast continual experiences of joy and praise and healing and prosperity?

Is it possible to be a Christian, to be respected, to outwardly manifest many characteristics we would quickly judge to be "spiritual," to be active in many spiritual activities and pursuits, and yet at the same time be building on wood, hay, and straw?

To get at an answer to these very important questions we need to look at a statement made by Jesus in Luke 6: "Why do you call me Lord, yet don't do the things which I say? . . . Whoever hears my words and does not do them, is like a man who built a house with no foundation. As soon as the river beat against it, the house fell immediately and its ruin was great" (vss. 47, 49, author's paraphrase). Throughout His teaching, Jesus states one measure of our spirituality—the *doing* of His words. And oddly enough (to our conditioned minds) those things He continually stressed usually have little or nothing to do with what is usually judged to be important in the Christian walk—our spiritual insights, our "ministry," our experiences. Throughout nearly everything He said, Jesus made it clear that serving others, laying down one's life for them in practical ways, was the measure of greatness in God's Kingdom. His instructions were very basic, down-to-earth. Look at some of them:

Do good to your enemies.
Treat everyone kindly.
Visit those in prison.
Don't judge.
Lend money when asked.
Feed the hungry.
Say your prayers in secret.
Forgive wrongs.
Go out of your way to help anyone in need.
Clothe those with no clothes.
Do good.
Show mercy.
Be kind.
Don't envy.
Don't speak critically.
Visit the sick.
Give abundantly.

Rejoice in everything.
Don't be pious in front of others.
Keep your mind pure.
Don't be angry.
Don't insult another.
Do to others what you would have them do to you.

The very familiarity of His words tends to keep us from seeing how astounding they really are. For how many of these things do most of us ordinarily equate with our spiritual growth? Usually we think of our growth and progress as a Christian in terms of what we are *learning and experiencing* rather than what we are *doing*. A great truth from the Bible bursts in upon us, we experience a marvelous healing, we feel the love of God in a deeper way as the result of some experience, we commit more aspects of our life to the Lord, we experience some significant new relationshp with another Christian, and after all these things we say, "The Lord is real to me, I am really growing closer to Him in exciting ways."

This is of course true and good. But we mustn't mistake this reality and these experiences for what Jesus clearly stated was the *true* nature of spiritual maturity—the *doing* of His words.

Therefore it is entirely possible for us in our day (as the Pharisees did in Jesus' day) to mistakenly spend our time and energy on things that for all outward appearances are spiritual, but which in the eternal value structure are hollow and passing and when subjected to the test of fire will burn as quickly as straw.

Throughout this book I have tried to emphasize two things: the *practical* ways we can prepare ourselves for the future, and the *ministry to others* such preparation will make possible. In light of Jesus' words, it is this service that is the highest example of building with gold, silver, and fine stones. Unless our lives are others-oriented, no matter how "spiritual," we are in grave danger of building with flammable materials. Every idea and suggestion in this book will be of no worth in your life whatever if you do not allow

God to use it to open you to other people's needs.

Separate, therefore, what is permanent from what is fleeting and temporary. Spend your life building with "real" stones. This will involve all of you, not merely the areas of life we have briefly discussed here. It will involve your daily obedience to God's instructions. It will involve every one of your relationships. It will involve your attitudes. The daily submission of your heart to God and the good you are able to build into the lives of others as a result—these are the things that remain.

Don't allow yourself to be caught in the tempting traps that turn so many Christians inward, fine things if they open your heart to God and others around you but which for so many end up being an end unto themselves—church activities, study, learning, experiences, worship, doctrines, books, healings, special revival meetings, miracles, praise, fellowship, denominations, Christian music, the gifts of the Spirit, witnessing, and even prayer. When these things become the focus rather than a means of turning us toward others they lose their meaning and turn to wood, hay, and straw.

You may follow the suggestions in this book right to the letter—exercise, eat well, fast, learn all sorts of useful skills, spend your money wisely, and learn to support yourself. But if you do not put all this to work to help and provide for others and to prepare you to be a servant more completely to those about you, nothing will have been gained. All your "preparation" will in fact be no preparation at all. It will be wood, hay, and straw.

Paul said it graphically:

If I speak in tongues . . . if I have prophetic powers . . . and understand all mysteries . . . and know everything there is to know . . . and have great faith . . . and give away all that I have . . . and should even give my body to be burned, but have no love, it amounts to *nothing*. (1 Cor. 13:1-3, author's paraphrase).

This is the standard of whether our stores be genuine. Seek out the real and do not confuse it with the passing.

This is more difficult to do than you might imagine. We are all guilty. We assume many things are eternal because they appear spiritual. But it is not always so. Unless our actions line up with the standards of behavior Jesus set, we are often building in vain.

This is the only way to spiritually prepare for the future. God is interested in a people who are willing to love and serve and who are capable of doing so through practice. Fasting and spending your money wisely won't necessarily make you capable of serving in that manner. But through your obedience in all these specific areas, God can teach you to build into the lives of people by serving them. All our efforts must spring from the motivation to turn our eyes from ourselves toward others.

Our preparation for the future is a calling to ministry.

Appendix I

PREPARING FOR THE FUTURE
IF YOU'RE NOT CHRISTIAN

This has clearly been a book for Christians. And I doubt there will be many of you who have read the entire book who are not. The things we have been discussing have been largely "family matters," and it has been my assumption that I was speaking to the rest of God's body.

However, if you presently are not in God's family I should make it clear to you that it is only as a Christian that you can hope to prepare for the future at all. For everything coming to the world in the future is intrinsicly woven together in God's ultimate plan for the universe. The single most important event in the entire history of mankind yet to occur is the return of Jesus to earth. When that time comes the people of the world will have already divided themselves into two groups: God's people and the others. Satan's grip on the world system and men's lives will be strong and only those who are submitted to God daily will have any chance of resisting his devices.

Therefore, unless you are a Christian who is walking day-by-day according to the principles of God, all other forms of attempted preparation for those times are fruitless.

Anyone can become a Christian. There is a special procedure, but there is no entrance standard. If you would like to be a Christian and thereby prepare yourself for the remainder of your life in the most meaningful way of all, here are some things you must do to join the family.

Paul said in Acts 16:31, "Believe on the Lord Jesus Christ and you will be saved." And in one sense that's all there is to becoming a Christian and then living as a Christian—believing.

Believing, however, is not nearly so simple as it sounds. In the Bible, the word meant considerably more than simply accepting certain facts and tenets as true—holding an opinion as we now use the word today. It was an active word, implying a total way of life—relying on, having confidence in, trusting, submitting to, obeying. You will even find hints of this more total definition in some of the older dictionaries.

A belief in Jesus then is not something we merely acquire the moment we intellectually say, "Okay, *I believe* in you—that you lived, that you died in my place, and that you possess the power to give me a new life now." To say this is good, it is a necessary step toward belief, but you have not yet arrived on the basis of this statement. Believing in Jesus has two sides: turning *away* from sin, self, the world, the devil *to* a new way of life, trust in and obedience to Jesus. This is the meaning of the word *"repentance."*

You must study the life of Jesus in order to do what He said. From such a study comes the process of *being* a Christian, *doing* what Jesus said, following His example, obeying His instructions, modeling your life after His.

That is what being a Christian is—believing in Jesus and obeying Him. You can begin the process of belief immediately by simply saying to God, "I recognize my need for You because I have up till now been going my own way apart from You. I realize that I am in God's eyes a sinner in rebellion. I repent of my sin and ask for Your forgiveness, for Jesus' sake. As an act of faith I now lay down control of my life and give it to You. Come into my life by Your Spirit and work there. Help me to learn Your will and then to do it. Help me to trust and obey You every day for the rest of my life. As I have now taken this step of the will, help me to fully and actively believe in You from this moment on."

By praying that prayer you are born into God's family, you become a Christian and the Spirit of God actually enters your being. That step is the door into a new way of life which will eventually claim every bit of you. Without going in for the full treatment, without living as Jesus instructed and submitting to God's will in your life, it will mean very little. Jesus and Paul and the other New Testament writers equated Christianity with a way of life, standards of behavior, not a list of intellectual beliefs.

Once you do become a Christian you must faithfully do several things in order to properly cement the change and to begin the lifelong process of following Jesus as an *active* believer. Most important you need to study the Bible, especially the Gospels, to find out precisely how a Christian is to live. (Use a modern translation.) For now that you are a Christian you cannot live any way you choose. There are instructions for us there and you must dig them out, apply them to your own life, and then carry them out.

To help you in this process you should begin to read (regularly) books by Christian authors. Go to your local Christian bookstore and browse among the shelves. I recommend one of the best to start off with is C. S. Lewis' *Mere Christianity and* I have written *Does Christianity Make Sense?* (Scripture Press) which will also be helpful. Both deal with the basics of being a Christian. From that point on there is an exciting world of Christian reading awaiting you on every conceivable topic.

You also need to meet with other Christians. Find a church where people are living the life of Jesus and are excited about it. Go ahead and be a little selective; some churches are stuck in the ruts of their traditions and do not exhibit this *life*. Talk to other Christians, pray with them, join a small Bible study group. You are now in a family and God's people function as a body.

There is true freedom in living as a child of God. These are not legalistic demands, but these things will help you understand what a Christian means and will help you to *do* what Jesus said.

Appendix II
PRIORITIES

I mentioned earlier that the suggestions in this book are not intended as any gauge of spirituality. I want to strongly re-emphasize that once again. I think this is important because it often is easy for us to become excited about new things and stress them to the degree that we lose a sense of balance and perspective in our lives. I find that tendency in myself and want to warn you of it as well.

We are all at unique stages of development, growth and maturity as Christians. And simply as human beings we are at different stages of life. We will therefore not always be in the process of following the same pursuits, being interested in the same things, or being led in similar directions. This says nothing about the validity of our personal relationship with God. It simply reveals the tremendous diversity of God's individual plans for each of us. For a Christian football player to disregard fasting during the fall months does not mean his commitment to the Lord and his preparation for the future are lacking. It just means he is a wise man who understands some things about his body and the rigors of the game.

Similarly, I do not encourage my wife to get out and run every day or to fast regularly. We have three children under age three and as I evaluate our priorities I realize that those three little boys need Judy far more than she needs exercise and fasting. There will be time for those things later on.

All these things we have discussed must be considered with respect to one's family, one's job, and other commitments. I don't mean to soft-peddle the importance of specific preparations for the future. I simply want to remind you to keep your eyes fixed on the overall goal, not certain specific aspects of it to the exclusion of everything else.

Most of these things can easily be incorporated into your regular routine. And they should be. But don't carry them to the extreme where they take you away from your family. Make your eating, fasting, gardening, learning skills, living on a budget, and exercise all family activities. Remember, these preparatory measures are intended to prepare us as a family, as a body, not as separate individuals.

Appendix III
HIGHLY RECOMMENDED
FURTHER READING

This has admittedly been a different sort of book. I have gathered together a series of seemingly unrelated topics under one roof and said, "Do these things to be faithful to God, to be wise stewards over His blessings, and to prepare for the future."

The wide range of topics discussed demanded brevity. Hundreds of books have been written on gardening, child raising, finances, and healthy eating. Yet here each of those topics was covered in just a few pages.

Yet there may linger in some of your minds suspicions about some of the statements I made because of this inadequate supportive evidence. It is not that my contentions are not well documented in other books by leading authorities. I simply chose not to lengthen this book hopelessly and to bog down your reading with hundreds of footnotes and many long quotes.

For instance, I said, "Sugar and white flour are bad for your system"; "persecution and deprivation are coming to America"; "our economy is decaying rapidly"; "fasting cleans out your body"; "you can save by living on a budget"; and "exercise will strengthen your heart." And you may have reacted to all these statements by thinking, "So *you* say. But how do I *really* know? Where's the proof?"

That's what I now intend to offer you here—evidence from many other sources about the things I've said. I want to point you in the direction of other books which cover in much more detail many of the topics we had only a chance to touch upon. And even this bibliography lists only a few out of hundreds of books on these topics. Seek out books on your own. Study. Dig for answers.

PART I

The Late Great Planet Earth—Lindsay (Zondervan)
The Vision—Wilkerson (Revell)
Racing Toward Judgment—Wilkerson (Revell)
The Feast of Tabernacles—Warnock (Bill Britton, Box 707, Springfield, Mo.)
The Day the Dollar Dies—Cantelon (Logos)
Money Master of the World—Cantelon (Logos)
Prophecy for Today—Pentecost (Zondervan)

PART II

Hidden Art—Schaeffer (Tyndale House)
Any books on gardening by the Rodale Press, Emmaus, Pa.—usually available at most Health Food Stores

PART III

Chapter Six

Let's Try Real Food—Renwick (Zondervan)
How to Eat Right and Feel Great—Rohrer (Tyndale House)
How to Eat Your Way Back to Vibrant Health—Kirban (Harvest House)
Are You Confused—Airola (Health Plus, Box 22001, Phoenix, Arizona)
None of These Diseases—McMillen (Revell)
Jesus Wants You Well—Lovett (Personal Christianity)
Help Lord, the Devil Wants Me Fat—Lovett (Personal Christianity)

Health Guide for Survival—Kirban (Kirban)
Let's Cook it Right—Davis (New American Library)

Chapter Seven

God's Chosen Fast—Wallis (Christian Literature Crusade)
How to Keep Healthy and Happy by Fasting—Kirban (Riverside)
Are You Confused?—Airola (Health Plus)
Help Lord, the Devil Wants Me Fat—Lovett (Personal Christianity)

Chapter Eight

Jesus Wants You Well—Lovett (Personal Christianity)
The New Aerobics—Cooper (Bantam)
Jog for Your Life—Gilmore (Zondervan)

Chapter Nine

"The Importance of Decision" (Cassette Tape)—Derek Prince (Christian Growth Min.)
"The Ministry of Management"—Campus Crusade; a course in planning & decision making
Managing Yourself—Douglass (Campus Crusade for Christ)

PART IV

Your Money Matters—MacGregor (Bethany)
There Is a Solution to Your Money Problems—Galloway (Gospel Light)
You Can be Financially Free—Fooshee (Revell)
Christian Financial Concepts, a workbook—Burkett (Campus Crusade)

PART V

The Christian Family—Christenson (Bethany)
A Christian Family in Action—Phillips (Bethany)
Dare to Discipline—Dobson (Tyndale House)
Hide or Seek—Dobson (Revell)
Blueprint for Raising a Child—Phillips (Logos)
The Effective Father—MacDonald (Tyndale House)

PART VI

Growth of a Vision—Phillips (Sunrise Books, 707 E St., Eureka, Ca.)
Mere Christianity—Lewis (Macmillan)
The Mark of the Christian—Schaeffer (InterVarsity)
The Greatest Thing in the World—Drummond (Revell)
Cry of the Human Heart—Ortiz (Creation House)

These books are ones I am familiar with and know are good. Most of them are sold in our store and are written from a Christian perspective. But you can find any number of helpful books on these topics in secular bookstores and health food stores as well.

NOTES

1. *Racing Toward Judgment* by David Wilkerson. Fleming H. Revell Co., Old Tappan, N.J., p. 8.

2. From *The Late Great Planet Earth* by Hal Lindsay. Copyright 1970 by the Zondervan Corporation. Used by permission, p. 43.

3. *The Vision* by David Wilkerson. Fleming H. Revell Co., Old Tappan, N.J.

4. Taken from *Hidden Art* by Edith Schaeffer. Copyright 1971 by Edith Schaeffer. Used by permission of Tyndale House Publishers, pp. 28-29.

5. From *Let's Try Real Food* by Ethel Renwick. Copyright 1976 by the Zondervan Corporation. Used by permission, pp. 25-26.

6. *The Prevention Method for Better Health* by J. I. Rodale. Rodale Books, Inc., Emmaus, Pennsylvania, pp. 118-128.

7. Op. Cit. *Let's Try Real Food*, pp. 44-46.

8. *El Molino Best Recipes Cookbook*. Copyright 1953 by El Molino Mills, p. 300.

9. Op. Cit. *Let's Try Real Food*, pp. 50, 52.

10. Taken from *How to Eat Right and Feel Great* by Virginia and Norman Rohrer. Copyright 1977 by Tyndale House Publishers, Wheaton, Ill. Used by permission, pp. 171-172.

11. Ibid., pp. 172-174.

12. Ibid., pp. 85, 87.

13. *Are You Confused?* by Pavvo Airola. Health Plus Publishers, Phoenix, Arizona, p. 107.

14. *Health Guide for Survival* by Salem Kirban, Salem Kirban, Inc., Huntingdon Valley, Pennsylvania.

15. *How I Conquered Cancer Naturally* by Eydie Mae, Harvest House Publishers, Irvine, Ca.

16. Op. Cit. *Are You Confused?*, p. 106.

17. *Shaping History Through Prayer and Fasting* by Derek Prince. Fleming H. Revell Co., Old Tappan, N.J.

18. *God's Chosen Fast* by Arthur Wallis. Christian Literature Crusade, Fort Washington, Pennsylvania.

19. *Jesus Wants You Well* by C. S. Lovett. Personal Christianity, Baldwin Park, California, pp. 239-241.

20. Reprinted by permission from *Your Money Matters* by Malcolm MacGregor. Published and copyright 1977, Bethany Fellowship, Inc., Minneapolis, Minn., p. 33.

21. Taken from *The Effective Father* by Gordon MacDonald. Copyright 1976 by Tyndale House Publishers, Whaton, Ill. Used by permission, pp. 13-15.

22. See also *Growth of a Vision* by Mike Phillips. Sunrise Books, 707 E St., Eureka, Ca.